HOW TO FIX YOUR **SH*T**

This book was a true labour of love. In fact, this book wasn't even meant to exist. It was a series of conversations in my head that I was struggling with.

The book I was meant to write, the one my publishers had signed off on, was on a totally different subject altogether. Then, six months after my deadline had passed, I still hadn't written *that* book.

This was more than writer's block. That book, the one I was supposed to write, had vanished into thin air.

I realized over a series of challenging days and weeks that my struggle wasn't in the writing; my struggle was in the content.

I had a book, this book, that needed to be written, and it was right in front of my eyes, yet all the while I was focused on writing *that* book. Doing the same thing over and over again, but nothing was working. was getting nowhere, fast. Sound familiar?

I realized that what I needed to do, what I *had* to do, was write the book in my head, the book in my heart.

The one that meant the most to me.

This is for you. You've got this. And I've got you.

ABOUT THE AUTHOR

Sháá Wasmund, MBE, is the author of the number one bestsellers *Do Less, Get More* and *Stop Talking, Start Doing*. She has been a lifelong supporter of encouraging more women into business. In 2015 Sháá received an MBE for her services to business and entrepreneurship. She was recently named one of the Top 20 Most Influential Entrepreneurs in the UK by the *Sunday Times*.

Today she runs one of the biggest and most active business Facebook Groups in the UK, The Freedom Collective, and has built a multi-million-pound online business from her back garden. Over the last five years Sháá has completely revolutionized how she works, and today she is proudly able to take seventeen weeks' holiday a year . . . albeit not all in the Maldives or Marrakesh!

Sháá inspires positive action with her no-nonsense, no-excuse advice and has made it her mission to help as many women as possible to create a life and business on their terms.

HOW TO
FIX
YOUR SH*T

A STRAIGHTFORWARD GUIDE
TO A BETTER LIFE

SHÁÁ WASMUND

PENGUIN LIFE

UK | USA | Canada | Ireland | Australia
India | New Zealand | South Africa

Penguin Life is part of the Penguin Random House group of companies
whose addresses can be found at global.penguinrandomhouse.com.

First published 2019
001

Set in 10.34/14.07pt Avenir Next
Typeset by Jouve (UK), Milton Keynes
Printed and bound in Great Britain by Clays Ltd, Elcograf S.p.A.

A CIP catalogue record for this book is available from the British Library

ISBN: 978-0-241-43684-4

www.greenpenguin.co.uk

CONTENTS

INTRODUCTION

So when did life get *so* complicated?

As Dr Seuss said, 'Sometimes the questions are complicated and the answers are simple.'

It's as if it creeps up on us like a thief in the night, stealing away our joy, our freedom and our *joie de vivre* . . . Suddenly we are on one long merry-go-round, desperate to get off, to take a break, or even a breath.

We try to pinpoint a time when the overwhelm first took hold. Was it when we had kids, got a mortgage, a new job, a divorce . . .? But the truth is, we can't really find the exact time; we just woke up one day and there it was.

That sense of everything just being a little too much to manage all at once. Nothing seems simple any more. There are so many responsibilities and obligations. We don't know what to focus on first or where to direct our attention because everything and everyone is pulling at us.

We can't remember the last time we really switched off.

We wake up in the middle of the night to go to the toilet and the first thing we do is check our phone. We say yes to things we don't want to do out of obligation to people we're not even sure we're really that keen on. As a result, we never have enough time for the people who really matter to us. Crazy, isn't it?

We feel pulled from pillar to post. We're never quite holding it all together, at least not at the same time. If we're making our

3

career work, then our friends and families are suffering. If we've got our kids on track, then we feel like we're not focused enough on work. There never seems to be enough money to take the kind of holidays we really want. In fact, just finding the time or the money to go on holiday is starting to become a task in itself. As for our health – well, let's just say that seems to fall down our priority list. Or maybe not even make it on to the list.

Our dreams seem like a long-distant memory and today's reality is just getting through the week without a major upset or drama.

We feel that whatever we do, no matter how hard we work, we just can't get the needle to move in the right direction – or at least not for long enough for there to be lasting change.

If this sounds like you, you're not alone, I hear you – I've felt like that so many times – but I promise you, you can change things.

You see, if we are truly honest, most of us are guilty of simply doing the same thing, over and over again, and somehow expecting a different result.

You can either allow the situation to consume you OR you can use the situation as a catalyst for change. Sometimes it feels like being consumed might be the easiest option, but change is what you want, it's why you've bought this book, so let's do that. The best place to start? Right here. Right now.

As we grow up, we are told that anger isn't a positive emotion, but I tend to disagree: anger is a much more positive emotion than despair and, channelled in the right way, it can be an extremely powerful catalyst for change. Never take your anger or frustration out on others; instead, channel it into taking back control of your life and your future.

It's time to look at your neurological pathways because, at the moment, they are taking you down the WRONG path.

If you keep repeating patterns, nothing changes. If you're not willing to turn left instead of right, you will stay on the same path.

The truth is, what got you here won't get you there, the place where you want to be. If you want something to change, then you have to be prepared to actually change, not just rerun the same coping mechanisms that have got you exactly where you are right now. Which is not where you want to be . . .

All too often, the fear of what we really want from life is greater than our will to get it. So we keep wishing for it, but with no real hope of ever achieving it because we never really do anything different. It's not that you don't want to, it's just that you don't know how to. And if we are being honest, sometimes, you're a little scared to.

So, how do we change that?

It starts by being more self-aware.

Life doesn't need to feel so complicated and overwhelming. Bear with me, and I promise you, between you, me and this book . . . we're gonna change it.

WHO THIS BOOK IS FOR

This book is for you if . . .

* you've woken up one day and asked yourself, *When did my life get so complicated?!*

* you're not where you want to be. Or where you thought you'd be.

* you know you can do more, be more and deserve more.

* you feel like you've really tried to change things, but nothing seems to shift. At least not permanently.

* you're exhausted. And frustrated. With life, but mostly with yourself.

* you're fed up with making the same mistakes over and over again.

* you've realized you don't know how to fix everything and you're ready to try something new.

* you want your life and yourself back.

* you know the past doesn't equal the future.

* you're ready for more.

* you want to live the life that you desire, not a watered-down version of it.
* most importantly, you're ready to fix your shit.

This book is not for you if . . .

* you think that there is a magic pill and it will all miraculously get better by itself.
* you'd prefer your life to be different but you don't really *want* it enough to make any real effort.
* you're not prepared to change what you're doing or how you're doing it . . . even though it's getting you nowhere.
* you think that by reading this book alone, your life will change. It won't.
* you suffer from 'poor me' syndrome (see page 63) and aren't prepared to accept it or do anything about it.
* you're not ready to take responsibility for your own life.

If any or all of the above refers to you, please do not pass Go, do not read another page. Just send this book back for a full refund. You're not ready, and maybe you never will be.

If, on the other hand, you've been guilty of any or all of these in the past but you're finally fed up with listening to your own bullshit, then this book was written for you. Yes, you.

HOW TO USE
THIS BOOK

I know this sounds a little like an instruction manual and, well, that's because it kinda is!

You see, I want you to actually use this book, not just read it. No shelf development.

You need to work out what you need from this book and then take it, with both hands.

Dip in. Skip it. Do it.

You don't need to read this from beginning to end (although you can); you are free to dip in and out where you see fit. If you want to skip something and come back to it later, do so.

For most of you, not everything in this book will resonate with you, although, I'm sure if you read each chapter, there will be at least one thing that makes you go, *Oh, that's me.*

You might have your career sorted but your health sucks. Or maybe you have the best relationship in the world with your partner but you could really do with sorting out your finances. Or maybe you've run three marathons already this year but you've been wanting to run your own business but never actually done it.

NOTHING IN THIS BOOK WILL WORK - UNLESS YOU DO

It is my hope that this book will provide you with new ideas, tools, thoughts and techniques to start to fix your shit. Whatever and how much that may be.

However, I want to be really, really clear. If you don't do the work, nothing will work. But don't worry, it's going to be easier than you think. When you start to see results, you're going to want to do the work.

The best way to fix your shit is like eating an elephant: one chunk at a time. Not that I'm suggesting you eat an elephant, of course.

You are going to read things and nod your head in agreement. You will think to yourself, *That's me*, or *Why didn't I think of it like that?* As you read the book, I hope you will be inspired and motivated to make change, but motivation can be as passing as the night.

Even the best book can't compete with the day-to-day stresses you have in your life, or the curveballs it may throw at you, let alone any self-destructive coping mechanisms you may have developed over the years. You are going to need to take those in your stride the best you can.

What I can do is make you abundantly aware of what is likely to happen.

You will want to change, you really will. You will want to fix your shit and you'll start making steps towards doing so . . . and then life will get in the way.

Your old coping mechanisms and habits are way more persuasive than I could be this far away from you in a book, but remember, YOU are more powerful than them. You really are.

If I was sitting right next to you, I promise you, every time I saw your old habits sneaking up on you I'd kick them into touch. But I'm not, so you're going to have to do that yourself. The more you do it, the less they will appear.

I want you to be realistic and expect things to go wrong, expect to want to go back to your old ways, because that's your comfort zone. But your comfort zone will not get you where you want to go. It will not make you who you want to be. It will not give you the life you both desire and deserve.

Right, are we on the same page?

Whatever you are used to doing, however you are used to responding, you've got to learn to do something different. If you don't, nothing will change. I cannot make this any clearer. I promise you, NOTHING will change until you do.

I think you know that your old ways of dealing with things do not work, or at least not as well as you want them to. They're not making your life any better. They're not sorting your shit out. And that is why you are here.

Yes, you are going to fall, and you are probably going to fail, too, but you are also going to get back up and fix your shit. You're going to change your ways so when you fail, when you make a mistake, you are not going to retreat. You are going to get back up, take responsibility and go again. Whether it's in your business, your personal life or your fitness. Whether you want to give up drinking, start a business or start a whole new life, the same principles apply.

Turn the corner of this page over and, when you're in doubt, come right back here and read this again and again. As many times as you need to.

Discipline dominates motivation. Each and every time.

I got you.

DON'T WAIT FOR TOMORROW

The trick to getting the most out of this book is: when you read something that resonates with you and hits you in your solar plexus, DO IT. Like, ACT on it. IMMEDIATELY. Pick up the phone, make the call. Apologize. Apply for a promotion. Chuck out all the junk food. Throw away the cigarettes. And the alcohol. Set up your new company. Join a gym. Go for a run.

OK, I know some of these are much harder to do than others. I am not for one second suggesting that everything is as easy as flicking a switch. I know it's not, but it IS possible. For me and for you.

Just do it. Don't wait for tomorrow.

Don't sit and think about it. Don't let your monkey brain take over. You know, the one that swings through your mind, back and forth, restless, indecisive and confused. It's going to try to give you all the reasons why you shouldn't bother changing, why it's too hard, why it won't work. Don't listen to it. Not this time.

Now's the time to fix shit.

PART **1**

SELF-**AWARENESS**

SELF-AWARENESS REQUIRES UNDERSTANDING WHO YOU really are rather than buying into the notion of who you think you are. Or who others think you are. Or who you think you should be.

Who do you really want to be? What do you really want and need? What makes you really happy? Once you understand that, getting it becomes a whole lot easier.

Some people put themselves down so badly it's no wonder they can't get up. They are literally their own worst enemies. Other people set such ridiculous goals of who they think they should be, often based on other people's ideas for them, that they are bound to fall short. Life is hard enough without making it harder.

So it's time to be good to yourself, but it's also time to be ruthlessly honest.

Most of us, myself included, will have spent vast periods of our lives trying to be someone we're not – half the time, not even realizing we are doing it. We've been conditioned by society, our parents, our partners, our upbringing, our teachers and, worst of all, our own limiting beliefs, to believe that we should be a certain 'type' of person. That conditioning also sets our expectations for what we believe we are entitled to want or able to achieve in life.

You were good at maths at school, so everyone told you to work in the City or be an accountant. The fact that you loved being creative was never really a viable option. Or maybe both your parents were doctors so, of course, you should become one, too. Or maybe they had low-paid jobs and, like me, you grew up on a council estate so no one thought you'd amount to much. Your stall was set out in life before you even had a chance to build it.

If you weren't sporty at school, you might have a belief that you'd never be good at sports. I had severe asthma as a child and never thought I could be good at sports so, funnily enough, I wasn't. Fast-forward to my new-found love of fitness and I can shoot some mean hoops and run for miles, all because I became aware that my belief that I wasn't good at sports was not my actual reality.

If you've never had a lot of money, you may well be telling yourself stories that you will never have money. In which case, that will probably be true. But it doesn't have to be. Sorting out your money shit isn't about winning the lottery. It starts with sorting out your relationship with money and creating a better one, and then doing something about it.

As someone who grew up poor, one of the biggest drivers in my life has been creating financial stability. At an early age, I came to the conclusion that I couldn't make 'real' money doing what I loved. So, instead, I followed what I considered to be a more acceptable path by running a 'proper' business, even though it wasn't what I wanted to do, who I really was and I wasn't even really that good at it.

This belief caused one of my biggest regrets in life: not being my authentic self sooner. For many years, I played into the notion that I had to do things a certain way in order to be 'good enough'. I felt I had all these boxes that I had to tick just to be validated. When I look back on it now, it seems crazy. I mean, who was I looking for validation from? Taking board positions that I never really wanted just to prove that I *could*. Having offices, staff and investors in order to prove I was 'serious'. This just demonstrates how out of touch I was with myself, with my own self-awareness.

For years, I wanted to write, teach and speak, but my beliefs held me hostage to the lie that 'creatives can't make real money'. I didn't believe it was possible for me. I thought about all the creative people I knew who were struggling to pay the rent, let alone a mortgage, and there was no way I wanted to put myself in that situation, so I carried on doing things because I could and because I was OK at them, but not because I wanted to.

However, in January 2015, that all changed. I left everything I'd ever known: my business, my board positions and every penny of my salary. I took a giant leap into the unknown in fear-less pursuit of the life I truly wanted. The truth is, you have no idea what is possible, if you don't try. The more self-aware you become, the more you are not just likely but willing to try to do the things that you really want to do.

And yes, it was the best decision I ever made. Well, at least when it comes to business.

CHAPTER ONE
GETTING TO THE THRESHOLD

CAN YOU REMEMBER A TIME WHEN SOMETHING CHANGED in your life? Maybe you gave up smoking or left a bad relationship. Maybe you had a job you hated and, one day, you had just had enough and handed in your notice. Something changed in that moment: you made a decision and you acted on it. You stopped thinking about it or talking about it and DID something about it. You got to the threshold, the point where you could no longer bear the situation you were in. For the first time, you turned left instead of right. That time when, even though you wanted to keep doing the same thing, you knew fundamentally in that moment that you could no longer put up with it. I use the analogy of turning left instead of right because it represents to me how we spend so much of our lives living on autopilot. We arrive at our destination without even knowing how we got there.

The truth is, the quickest way to fix shit is to learn how to get yourself to that point, to that threshold, sooner.

Think back to what happened in those moments when something inside you changed. Maybe it was the proverbial straw that broke the camel's back, but something shifted. You went from wanting to change to changing.

EXERC*SE:
FINDING YOUR THRESHOLD

We've all been there before – wanted to change something for so long but, for whatever reason, it just wasn't happening, and then, all of a sudden, something shifted and it was like we changed overnight. This is your threshold. The point of no return.

My mum used to smoke, and she had tried to give up many times, but to no avail. She decided that she needed to get to that threshold quicker, so she took decisive action.

Every time she smoked, she put the cigarette butt in the fireplace in our living room. Soon enough, the stench became so great, so overpowering, so sickening, that she stopped. In that moment. The moment the smell of the old fag ends took over the house and all its inhabitants and our clothes. That was it.

Whenever I want to get to my threshold a little sooner, so I can stop wallowing and start making changes, I do a bit of visualization.

Try this . . .

Think of something you want to change. Let's take two different examples: 1) you want to change your job because it's not what you really want to do and, if you were truthful, you no longer enjoy it and 2) you want to lose some weight.

Let's start with your job. Now, imagine you stay in this job for the rest of your life. How much money will you be able to earn? What kind of life will that provide you with? How many hours a week, a month, a year will you spend commuting? How bored will you be? How much will you hate getting up on a Monday morning?

You get the picture? OK, so now let's list all the things that you could do to change this bleak scenario.

1. Update your CV
2. Gain some new skills
3. Sign up to some online courses
4. Apply for an internal promotion/role change
5. Apply to an entirely different company

I am sure you can add to the list but, when you look at it, it's pretty straightforward, right? And certainly a lot more enjoyable than spending the rest of your life in career purgatory.

Now let's tackle that extra 10lb (or 20lb, or whatever the figure is). Go put on a pair of jeans that you can no longer quite fit into – I don't mean a pair that you wore when you were nineteen but a pair that, if you were being honest, you really should (and want to) fit into now. Wear them around the house for the whole day . . . and now visualize how you will feel if you can fit back into these jeans with ease.

When you're trying to get to your own personal threshold faster, it's important to note whether you are a 'towards' or an 'away' person. As the legendary Tony Robbins teaches, we are all driven by either pain or pleasure. Do you want more of something, or less of it?

What will help you more in improving your health and fitness – visualizing a strong, fit body, or visualizing an unhealthy, overweight body that can't walk up the stairs?

Most of the time, I am a 'towards' person. So when it comes to my career or my finances, I am always looking towards greater pleasure (like in the example of losing weight above), but when it comes to my health and fitness, I'll be honest, I'm more driven by moving away from the visualization of being overweight and unfit. So picture both scenarios and you will soon see which one creates a more powerful reaction for you.

Now you know whether you are a 'towards' or an 'away' person, you can structure your scenarios accordingly, and this works just as well in your personal life as it does in business.

It's like foretelling the future, one way or the other.

In the moment you went from wanting to change to changing, you developed a new-found sense of purpose, determination and courage. You took action. You took the kind of action you'd been thinking about for a long time but had never been able to follow through on. Until that moment.

That moment when you reached a breaking point. The pain of not doing something became far greater than the pain of staying stuck. You found your threshold.

Now think about all the things you want to fix and ask yourself:

What will happen if I don't get this sorted? What are the ramifications, not just for now, but for my future?

Is this the example I want to set for myself, or for others?

Am I prepared to live with that, knowing that I had a choice?

Do I want to just stay stuck, or keep on keeping on?

I hope not. It's time to wake up from your slumber and get ready to make some changes. Once. And. For. All. I know it's so much easier to create an excuse than it is to create change, but that's not why you bought this book, so let's just get on with it, shall we?

CHAPTER TWO

HOW TO FIX YOUR SH*T

FIXING YOUR SHIT IS ACTUALLY MUCH SIMPLER THAN YOU think – really, it is – but you've got to start by tackling the real thing that is standing in your way, and yes, my friend, that's you.

Making any life-impacting decision is only ONE step of the equation. Doing that without understanding how you got to that point or addressing how you want your future to be will NOT change anything long term. You may have a momentary win but, if you don't shift your mindset at the same time, those wins will be short-lived.

Making one small change and expecting overnight results doesn't work either. You need consistency.

Truth is, we all have shit to deal with, some of it the same, some of it different. And some people more than others.

That's just how life goes.

Some of us suffer in our personal lives, going from one bad relationship to the next. Others struggle with weight gain, spending their whole lives yo-yo dieting on one diet or another. For some, it's addictions. Maybe it started out as casual drinking but, over the years, as life got more complicated, the drinking has turned into a coping mechanism, but, ironically, it now just makes coping even harder.

Maybe your shit is knowing that there is so much more you want to do with your life but you simply don't know how. You're fed up with the way you've been living and feel like you're always coming up short.

For a lot of people, money – or the lack of it – is their biggest challenge. Earning it, keeping it, saving it and growing it. No matter how hard they seem to work, there's just never enough money at the end of the month. They worry about their pensions and how they are going to cope when they have no choice but to stop working.

Or maybe it's just that, deep down, you know that even though you're making decent money, have a decent job and a decent life, you're still not fulfilling your potential. I'm sure other people look at you and think you have it all sussed, but the truth for you is that you still feel like a fraud sometimes. You still feel like you're only half performing. I've been here – many, many times.

One thing's for sure: we almost all feel overwhelmed at some points in our life. If you're lucky, these points are fleeting but, for many people, the situation seems to hang around like a constant, dull headache. We try to pretend it's not there, take a few tablets and hope it will go away. It can feel like we're stuck in quicksand and, no matter what we do, nothing seems to get us out of it.

But this isn't about feeling sorry for ourselves or wallowing in the fact that we have *more* shit to deal with than our friends, neighbours, partners . . . or anyone else. This is about fixing it. Once. And. For. All.

If you didn't know how to fix it before, you will by the end of the book, I promise. It all starts with YOU. And that is a good thing, a great thing even, because it means you have the power to change everything.

First, you have to accept where you really are (at least for right now). You've got to stop the denial. And the hiding.

There is no shame in having shit to sort out. We all have.

However, I promise you one thing: without accepting what is really going on, where you are really at, nothing will get fixed.

EXERC*SE:
WHY WE MAKE EXCUSES

Right . . . the best way to stop making excuses is to start writing them down. Before you begin, I want to remind you that this exercise is for you and no one else. No one else needs to see all your excuses, but you do!

So, let's get started. I want you to take a pen and paper and write down ALL of your excuses, and I really do mean ALL of them. I want you to leave an empty line underneath each one.

Not sure where to start? Let me give you some ideas . . .

Why you don't go to the gym as much as you should? Why you haven't started that business yet? Why are you still holding on to friendships, or even a relationship, that you know you should have left a long time ago?

What about the simple daily excuses you make, for example that you don't have time to do x, y or z . . . I am sure, if you are anything like me, you will have a long list of these types of excuses. Or, at least, I used to. I still have a list, but it is a lot shorter now!

Once you've listed all your excuses, I want you to go to the empty line underneath each one. Look at the excuse in the cold light of day with a fresh pair of eyes and ask yourself:

Is this an emotional response?

What are you scared of?

Is this what you have always done?

Is this excuse even logical?

What would you rather have in the future?

Are you going to get what you want if you carry on believing this excuse?

For each excuse, I want you to write down an alternative. Even if, right now, you don't believe it's possible, there has to be an alternative. Write it down.

Now, each day, try practising the alternative for at least one of your excuses. I promise you, before you know it, your list will get shorter and shorter.

Sometimes when we are asked to do exercises like this we park them and think *I'll come back to this later*, but we rarely do. I'd really encourage you to put the book down, grab a notebook and start this excercise now.

When you start looking at things with a different perspective they start to change a lot quicker. Start with the task or the excuse that seems the easiest to change. Once you've got over that one, you'll find the rest easier to address.

CHAPTER THREE

ACCEPTING THE PRESENT DOESN'T MEAN ACCEPTING THE FUTURE

PLEASE BE CLEAR ABOUT THIS: YOUR REALITY, RIGHT NOW, does NOT define you. Whatever it is, it simply gives you the truth to work with. Life will not always be like this, whether it's big things holding you down or little things that annoy you. Maybe it's just a recognition that you could and should do more. Whatever it is, if it's important to you to change it, change it you will.

PART 2

MINDSET

WHEN YOU REALLY, REALLY WANT SOMETHING, NOTHING will stand in your way. Nothing. Not even yourself.

Motivation comes and goes. When it's there we get all fired up in a flurry of activity, but when it's not we hit the snooze button, just one more time. This is where having a robust mindset comes in. This is where the phrase 'Discipline dominates motivation' comes in. Discipline dominates motivation every time. That means, even when we don't want to do something we do it anyway.

Discipline is doing whatever is needed to get the result you desire, even when you don't feel like it any more.

That's how you start to fix your shit. First, by accepting the reality of your situation; second, by getting clear on what you really want in your life; and third, by finding the courage to do something about it. Look at the ways in which that behaviour, habit, job, relationship – whatever it is – is NOT serving you. Now ask yourself, what would be a better alternative?

Deep down, some people would prefer to fail. I know this sounds mad and a little abrasive, but please bear with me. I honestly believe that some people would prefer to fail – as long as it's not their own fault. As long as it's their situation or their 'circumstances'. Because if they fail, they can justify giving up, and giving up is far easier than constantly trying, not succeeding, picking ourselves up and trying again. But you know that's not the answer. Think instead about where you want to go and how you are going to get there. You are a trier and you will succeed. That is why you are reading this book.

People say they want something when, really, what they mean is it would be *nice* to have it, as long as they don't have to make themselves feel really uncomfortable in the process of getting it. Far too few of us are prepared to go outside of our comfort zones. Instead, we just keep doing what we've always done and keep getting the results we've always got – whether that's our personal relationships, our career projection, our business or our health.

You see, when you really, really want to succeed, when you really want to fix your shit, you have to go all out. You don't take no for an answer. You put blood, sweat and tears into it.

CHAPTER ONE
WANT VERSUS PREFER

WHEN MOST PEOPLE SAY THEY WANT SOMETHING, WHAT they really mean is that they would 'prefer' it. They would 'prefer' it if they lost weight; they would prefer it if they had a better relationship; they would prefer it if they gave up drinking; they would prefer it if they woke up every day loving their job and their life – but far fewer people are prepared to make the necessary changes in order to get it.

Until you reconnect with reality and accept who you are and where you are right now, nothing will change. Most people spend so much of their time detached from themselves and the reality of their situation that it seems almost like their lives are happening to someone else. They have become a bystander to their own lives, watching them crash in slow motion but without the courage to put the brakes on.

So how do you find that courage? The courage to say what you want. The courage to get what you want. The courage to fix your shit.

It starts by getting really clear on the things that we really, deeply care about and pursuing those with a vengeance. The rest – well, the rest can wait in line.

Too many people want things but never quite get them. They

always seem just that little bit out of reach. Trust me, I've been guilty of this, too. In the past, it would go something like this . . . It's cold and I'm tired, I really can't run or get in the car and drive fifteen minutes to go to the gym. I'd rather sit here and watch Netflix, but I'll pretend I'm being healthy by having a bowl of porridge and chopped-up dates. So I could tick a box in my head telling myself that I'm being good, even though I wasn't. I'd say, I can't focus on my fitness right now because it's not the right time, I'm not ready, I've got too much work on. I'm a single mum, I'm stressed, I'm tired. All of those things were true, but they were also bullshit. What I was doing was choosing what was easy over what I really wanted. You tell yourself that you haven't got the qualifications, the bank balance or the pedigree to get what you really want. So you settle. You tell yourself the thing you want is just not possible for you.

You really want to start up a business, but you stay in a job you don't even like because it's 'easier'. You really want to have a great relationship, but you either stay stuck in an unhappy one or stay by yourself for fear of committing to someone who would really matter to you because you are afraid of getting hurt. Deep down, however, you know the truth. The only thing that's really stopping you is you. As clichéd as it sounds, it's the truth.

As Gary Vaynerchuk says, 'Most people's actions don't match their complaints or their desires.' You tell yourself you don't have time, yet the reality is we all have exactly the same amount of time as each other. Life is far less complicated than we think it is. It's truly about the choices we make. Each day brings an opportunity to make new and better choices.

In short, let's stop doing the shit that doesn't matter with the people that don't matter. There is a very big difference between wanting something and preferring something, but many people get the two confused.

People *want* to lose weight but *prefer* to watch Netflix.

People *want* to get better jobs but *prefer* to drink after work rather than learn new skills.

People *want* a great relationship but *prefer* to settle.

The reality is that people aren't willing to go outside their comfort zone to get what they want, which means they don't really want it, they merely prefer it. My Achilles heel was my fitness. I just never prioritized it.

I would choose easy over what I really wanted. I wanted to be super-fit and strong, not just a particular 'size' . . . but I never put in the work. I *preferred* to be fit, but I didn't really *want* it.

The moment that switched in my brain, everything changed. The moment I decided I was no longer going to choose what was easy over what I wanted, even when it was difficult, my fitness completely transformed – you could say it metamorphosized.

And you know how long it took me? Ninety days. I lost over 20lb, increased my muscle mass, lost over 10 per cent of my body fat, increased my bone density . . . and turned my BMA (Base Metabolic Age) to that of a twenty-nine-year-old. PS: I'm not twenty-nine!

The body and mind are so powerful when you put them to work on positive things. Today, I am stronger, leaner and fitter than I was twenty years ago and I look better. Why? Because I decided to choose what I really wanted over what was easy. What was easy was to keep on snacking, what was easy was to stay inside instead of running in the rain. Did any of it get me what I wanted? Of course not. It kept me exactly where I was.

For sure, what you really want feels harder in the beginning but, in the long run, it's the only thing that will give you what you want. And the long run really isn't that long.

We all have a tendency to focus on what is the worst that could happen and completely overestimate how terrible that could be, and this tactic is also a great excuse for procrastination.

Other times we think we want something, but really all we've done is internalized someone else's goals – could be our parents', teacher's or partner's – and then we mistake them for our own. No wonder we don't pursue them with all our might – they're not even ours.

Or maybe they were ours once, but it was so long ago and we haven't even stopped to ask ourselves if this is really what we *still* want. People grow, they change and evolve and, as they do, so do their dreams.

Whether it's your personal life, your fitness or your career, it's your choice. You have a choice to be in a relationship that makes you truly happy and in a career that you love, and you have the choice to be the fittest you've ever been. Or you can stay stuck, carrying the extra pounds, never having enough money and remaining living a life that doesn't make you truly happy.

Your choice.

CHAPTER TWO

THINKING ABOUT
THE ALTERNATIVE

NOW THINK ABOUT ALL THE THINGS YOU WANT TO FIX and ask yourself this: What will happen if you don't get this sorted? What are the implications, not just for now, but for your future? Remember the exercise you did on getting to your threshold sooner? Apply that here. What happens if you do get this sorted, and what happens if you don't? Really feel the ramifications; don't just theorize them.

Remember: indecision is a decision. You are forever at the mercy of others, with no control over your own life or business. Indecision is a choice. Make a better one.

Said things you regret? Fallen out with someone you love? Know you're in the wrong? Does it even matter? Reach out, apologize, before you don't have the chance to. Think of that person and imagine never being able to have that conversation with them. How would you feel? How would that impact your life?

It's a small thing to do, but one that could make a big difference to you. And something you could do right now.

CHAPTER THREE

YOU'RE NEVER GOING TO BE COMPLETELY FEARLESS

'COURAGE IS NOT THE ABSENCE OF FEAR,
BUT THE ABILITY TO CONTINUE IN SPITE OF FEAR . . .'

- NELSON MANDELA

EVER FEEL LIKE THE COWARDLY LION IN *THE WIZARD OF OZ*?
Deep in your heart, you know exactly what you want and need to do, but you just can't seem to find the courage to do it. Fear takes over and stops you in your tracks.

The first thing to accept is that you are never going to be fearless. It's about how we deal with fear.

Fear is a lot like a bully: you've got to knock it down to remove its power. Imagine fear as a balloon and courage like a pin . . . All you need to do is tap that balloon with a bit of courage and – *poof!* – it's gone. Of course, this is easier said than done, but stick with the theory. It works.

There are many times in our lives when we should be fearful but, instead, courage takes over. I remember when I found out that my best friend's boyfriend was going to a wedding . . . with someone else. I had to decide whether to tell her, ignore the information or do something about it. Well, like I do with most things, I decided to do something about it and confront him head on. So I drove five hours to the wedding, searched him out and confronted him outside the party.

This guy was six foot two; I'm five foot four. He's a black belt in jiu-jitsu and a lawyer. I'm not. But I had courage on my side.

I gave him the choice: if he didn't tell my friend himself within twenty-four hours, I would.

I'm pretty sure he wanted to punch my face in – it certainly looked like it – but I reminded him that, if he did so, he would be disbarred and lose his job, not to mention being locked up for a while. Now I'm not going to lie, I was more than a little fearful, but when it comes to protecting the people I love, my courage outweighs my fears ten to one.

I also remember being suspended from primary school at nine years old. My best friend, Valerie, was being bullied during playtime. A group of girls had surrounded her and were taunting her with racist remarks (she's Jamaican); there were six of them, only one of her. I don't even remember being fearful, I just remember wanting to protect my friend, so I ran in and pushed the biggest girl to the floor and stood in front of Valerie. I was dragged to the principal's office (I lived in California at the time) and told that I was being suspended for starting a fight. I tried to defend myself, but the principal wasn't listening.

Fortunately, my mum had greater powers of persuasion than I did at that point and reminded him that she was a journalist and, unless he wanted to be outed for condoning racism, he needed to look at the situation again, as I had simply been defending my friend. Suffice to say, I was back at school the next day and the other girls were suspended.

Now I'm not saying this to advocate violence of any kind. I don't. However, I do believe we all have far more courage inside us than we might think; sometimes, you just need to be put into a situation that requires you to find it. We are almost always more courageous when it comes to doing right by other people than we are to doing right by ourselves.

The same applies to our working lives. When was the last time you applied for a job outside your comfort zone or really tried something new in your business? But I bet when your friends talk about promotions or new ideas you actively encourage them. You'll be the first to cheer lead and offer any practical advice and help that you can, yet there are *still* things in your life, your career and your business that you *really* want to do, but have been putting off because you're too scared to try.

Take the courage you have to look after, defend and champion others and to embrace it for your own life. Step out of your comfort zone. Do something different. Push yourself when it doesn't feel comfortable. Go for the promotion; the one you really want, not just the one you think you'll get. Start the new business or even close the business. Sometimes leaving something is as scary as starting it.

'IT TAKES COURAGE TO GROW UP AND
BECOME WHO YOU REALLY ARE.'

– E. E. CUMMINGS

CHAPTER FOUR

USING YOUR EMOTIONS TO MAKE A CHANGE

IT'S TIME TO FIND SOME EMOTIONS STRONGER AND MORE powerful than fear . . . like anger or hope and, most certainly, courage. I truly believe that when anger and frustration (a lesser form of anger) are channelled in a positive direction, they are extremely powerful. Get angry at the fact that fear has affected your ability to live the life you want to live or be the person you know you can be. Get angry at yourself for not doing anything about it sooner. Yes, I totally believe in being kind to ourselves, but lying to ourselves isn't being kind. It's just lying. It's the opposite of being kind to yourself, as it lulls you into a false sense of security that your life is just fine, when really you know you're short-changing yourself.

Accept where you are and that only you can change it. Use that anger and frustration with yourself to create momentum, because it's sure as hell better to change today than to go on like this for ever.

In almost every situation, our brains are hard-wired to think of the worst possible outcome. We often allow fear, ego and pride to rule our lives. We're afraid we're going to look foolish, so we don't try. We're afraid it won't work, so we don't try. We're afraid we're going to f*ck up again, so we don't try.

We don't lack solutions; we lack the courage to pursue them.

CHAPTER FIVE

WE ARE ALL CAPABLE
OF CHANGE

IT'S INCREDIBLE HOW MUCH WE CAN CHANGE IN A REALLY short period of time once our minds are set on doing so. We are all capable of turning our personal lives, our work, our health and our fitness around. Really we are. I transformed my fitness in ninety days. This is a totally realistic and effective timeframe to replace bad habits with good ones. It's enough time to lose a significant amount of weight, to start a business and get clients, to learn a new language, to rewire your brain's coping mechanisms . . . and make a few slip-ups along the way. Because that will happen, too, trust me!

When I set up my current business, I had no idea what I was doing, but I started anyway. Of course, I made a fair few mistakes, but ninety days in and I was much closer to where I wanted to be. More importantly, I was finally doing what I loved. Same was true for my fitness. When I started out, running was soooo hard (I had asthma) and there were many, many times I was tempted not to run, but I was committed to it. So I did it. Was it perfect? Absolutely not. Many days, I only ran one mile instead of the three-mile target I set myself, but I still did it.

I kept up the good habit, even if it wasn't perfect. Crazily enough, I now love running.

Human beings are amazing creatures and every day we wake up is truly a new opportunity to change and grow into the person we want to be.

CHAPTER SIX

LUCK HAS NOTHING
TO DO WITH IT

ONE OF MY PET BUGBEARS IS PEOPLE CALLING ME, OR anyone else, lucky. Unless they've won the lottery, in which case, they *are* lucky. But even then, you have to be in it to win it.

I hear things like:

'Wow, Sháá, you're so lucky to get to do the work that you love.'

'You're so lucky you've had three number-one bestsellers.' (Fingers crossed this makes it four!)

'You've got such a great lifestyle. I wish I could have that.'

Er, OK, do you think luck made all that happen?

We need to stop telling ourselves these stories that some people are luckier because they had a better education, or they look or sound a certain way, or they had wealthy parents. You know what, I think those perceived advantages can be a disadvantage, because they remove the hunger and the reason to hustle. It might look easier, but I'm not sure it is.

When we look at other people's lives from the outside, we make all kinds of assumptions, and almost all of them are incorrect. We do both them and ourselves a disservice. Them,

45

because more often than not they have worked damned hard for their 'luck'; and ourselves, because we are assuming that this is not possible for us, that's it's purely down to a force we can't control.

One of the people I admire greatly is a man called David Goggins. On first look, you'd think he'd had it easy: good-looking guy, ex-Navy SEAL and probably one of the fittest men on earth. But that's what you see on the surface. David grew up in an incredibly violent household where he was beaten up on a weekly, if not daily, basis. He was constantly bullied for the colour of his skin and referred to as 'nigger' for much of his childhood at school. With no solace at home, he withdrew into himself, but one day he got to his threshold, and the turning point for him was watching a Navy SEAL training video. He just decided in that moment that enough was enough. At 300lb, he was told that he wasn't fit enough to make it through the training. Rather than give up, Goggins literally transformed himself by losing 110lb in less than three months.

Goggins is the poster child for fixing his shit, no matter the circumstances. The most incredible story for me is when he decided with a week to spare that he was going to run the San Diego One Day race . . . and this isn't some 10k afternoon run, it's a twenty-four-hour race over 100 miles. He wanted to start running ultramarathons to raise money for charity and, in order to do so, he had to qualify. The San Diego race was the first race he could enter, but one small thing: he had never run a marathon, let alone an ultramarathon, and weighing in at 250lb (at that point of sheer body-building muscle), he was not built for it either. After 70 miles, his body gave up. All the metatarsal bones in his feet were broken and, unable to make it to the toilet, he was peeing blood down his legs. This would be enough for almost all of us to give up, but Goggins is convinced that, at the point we are ready to give up, we have at least 40 per cent left. He wrapped his ankles in tape, visualized himself as someone who perseveres, no matter what the challenges, and conjured in his body the adrenaline he needed. Those last 30 miles, he didn't stop once. When you hit a wall, he says, remember that most walls have doors, you just need to find a way through.

Here are some personal home truths when it comes to 'luck'.

I started working every weekend when I was thirteen and have worked ever since. I grew up in a single-parent family on a council estate in the UK and was the first person in my family to go to university. Nobody gave me luck or anything else because they simply didn't have it to give.

I wouldn't change a thing. It made me make my own luck.

I am grateful for what I have, but I don't think I'm lucky. I lost my partner, my son's dad, when my son was only three and a half. I don't call that luck. I'd swap everything I have to turn back time, but I can't.

I've been a grafter my whole life, and hard work often gets mistaken for luck. I've worked since I was a teenager. I've done everything, cleaned hospital toilets; and although I've never drunk alcohol, I've served drinks in a bar; and washed dishes by hand in crappy restaurants – but I never complained.

It's not always about what you want to do, it's about what you have to do.

So if I needed money, I needed to go to work, and it didn't matter if I was stacking shelves or cleaning toilets. I would do whatever I could do until I could do something better. I would never look down on something when I needed money and think to myself, *That's beneath me, I'm not doing that*. So much so that, vegetarian since my teens, I even fried hamburgers in McDonald's. Ego and pride can stand in the way of 'luck'. They stop us creating our own luck because sometimes we feel that it should be easier, or that we shouldn't need to be doing the things that we do just to get by. Maybe it should be easier, maybe we shouldn't have to juggle so much or take jobs we don't want, but if that's going to get us closer to what we want, then I'm the first in line.

As Gary Vaynerchuk says, 'You can keep that luck shit in your pocket.'

Bizarrely, I won a McDonald's scholarship while at university, so they paid my tuition fees. Now, I know some of you may be thinking, *That's a sell-out*, and maybe it is – when you have the privilege of choice. Maybe a vegetarian shouldn't have taken up the scholarship, but when I weighed up not taking it against £20,000 in tuition fees, I decided that my personal morals, at least for the time being, needed to take a back seat.

As part of the scholarship programme, I had to go and work in the restaurants, going in on the ground floor. That didn't mean I could carry on frying hamburgers, though. In fact, this is precisely where my 'luck' started. I was eighteen, living in a tiny studio flat in north London and going to work at McDonald's in Leicester Square, the busiest in the country, six days a week, for six weeks. What I learned during this time was that luck is in the hustle and the grind and the graft. It's not in the sitting back, accepting your 'lot' and complaining. It's not in the 'poor me' syndrome. It's not the 'I don't really want to do that' or 'I need to wait for the right time'.

There is no such thing as the right time or the right moment, there is just the here and now. If you need money, you've got to figure out a (legal) way of making it. If the job you've got right now isn't enough, do something else as well. In this world, there is always something else you can do.

I had been frying burgers for all of five days when I realized, getting on the train home, that the manager, Leroy, was getting in the same carriage. Never one to be shy, I went and sat next to him. I can't pretend I had some grand plan back then, I didn't, but I am always genuinely interested in people. I asked him about his job, what he loved and what he hated. Turned out, he hated doing the weekly reports and, well, I'm kinda good at things like that. Enter luck. I offered to write up the weekly reports – and that was the last time I had to fry hamburgers. Nice trade. Win–win.

I've never drunk alcohol in my life – not for any particular reason; it just never appealed to me. When the only job I could find was working in a bar, guess what I did? I worked in a bar. I'm not sure you would have wanted the drinks I was mixing; it was a bit like a vegetarian cooking chicken . . . you're never really sure about the end result! The point is that luck is something that you get and make from working hard, from hustling, from grabbing opportunities, from being a good person and being kind.

Somebody whose life you impacted five years ago could be the very person who opens the biggest door for you in the future. I truly believe in karma. Maybe I'm a bit more 'woo woo' than I care to admit. I'm constantly thinking of all the people who have helped me out over the years and how I can help others by paying it forward.

I know I've been in some situations in life that some people would describe as 'lucky', like when I landed a job at just twenty-one to work with the legendary former Super Middleweight Boxing Champion Chris Eubank. Am I grateful for that and to him? Without a doubt. Was it luck? Hell, no.

Luck is something you create; it's not something that is given to most people. There is no magic fairy dust, there's no wand. You have to go out and create it.

When I was in my second year at university I won a competition to write for *Cosmopolitan* and, one day, while I was sitting in the editor's office, staring at a big pile of letter-headed paper on her desk, a crazy thought entered my head. As a mad boxing fan, I thought to myself, what if I was to interview the boxer Chris Eubank for the magazine? Well, there was only one way to find out. So I absconded with five sheets of the letter-headed paper. I was hustling way back before anyone even used the word 'hustle'.

I wrote Chris Eubank a letter, saying that I was doing an article for *Cosmo*, because the truth is, in my naivety, I genuinely thought that they would take it. Chris agreed to the interview and I had to go back and confess to the editor. She just looked at me and said, 'Sháá, you are crazy! You must be the only female in the country who is interested in boxing! None of my readers will want to read this!' I wanted to die. Then she looked at me and said, 'But I admire your initiative, so let me see what I can do.' She picked up the phone, called a colleague and sold the story to a national newspaper, which meant I could pay off the student loan I'd taken out to cover my rent. Was I lucky to have won the competition to write for *Cosmo*? Maybe a little bit, but I'd like to think my writing had something to do with it and, if I hadn't entered, I'd never have won. Was I lucky to get the interview with Chris Eubank? Well, again, kind of. I mean, he could have said no, but I used my initiative and I hustled hard.

Chris was two hours late for the interview, and then I had to wait, sitting in on an interview with a journalist from a famous tabloid. She was furious. The interview was more like a boxing match; she berated him non-stop and, after forty-five minutes, she literally walked out. Thinking I was a 'proper' journalist, Chris turned to me and asked me what he had done wrong, expecting some seasoned advice. Oh, the naivety of youth! I just told him the truth as I saw it.

'Chris, I don't know why you did that interview. That's her style, that's what she does to people.' So he just looks at me and he says, 'Do you want a job?' I said yes before I had any idea what I was saying yes to.

I was entering my last year at the London School of Economics and everybody else in my peer group was hell bent on becoming a banker. I had no idea what the job was and I had no idea how I was going to finish my degree. I also recognized a once-in-a-lifetime opportunity.

Luck is where you grab an opportunity and turn it into something. It's hard work and determination. Don't get me wrong: hard work and determination don't always pay off, and I am no exception. Plenty of things have not panned out the way I wanted in my life, despite hard work and determination. But here's the thing, to use a boxing analogy:

It's not how you get knocked down that counts,
it's how you get back up.

Consistency also creates luck. Consistency in always doing what you say you will when you say you will. The consistency of over-delivering and being reliable.

Apparently, good things just happen to 'lucky' people. They have an idea, then they just go and do it and it works. Right? Wrong. What actually happens is that the people who work hard and believe in what's possible and rethink their own possibilities, they go and *try* it. It doesn't always work, but it's what they learn from it that makes the next idea work.

Let me tell you what unlucky people do.

Unlucky people sit and talk about the idea and the concept for another six months while never doing anything to take a single step towards that goal. They might tweak a logo and then tell you the 101 reasons why they're stressed out and why they can't get this started right now, or at least not until x happens, or maybe it's y – who knows? But it's always something.

You've got to jump out of the plane and build your wings on the way down. You have to just jump. You have to do things, not just talk about doing them. You build your wings and you build your luck in the process of doing it. You don't build your wings or your luck while you're overthinking and procrastinating about things. You build it by doing and falling and picking yourself back up again.

What people who call people like me lucky think is that I've never fallen. They don't see all my bruises or scars, but I have so many of them. To me, they're the scars of life. They show that I was prepared to live fully. To love fully. I was prepared to play full out in everything and everyone that I was a part of, because what other option is there?

Every time you get back up, you're going to win and succeed far more than the person who is still sitting there talking about their ideas, their plans, their dreams, their problems but doing nothing about it. They will sit in their armchair talking about you and me and people like us and say how 'lucky' we are.

They say luck is what happens when preparation meets opportunity, but I think it's more than that. If you prepare in your office, in isolation, but never put yourself or your ideas out there into the world, well, nothing is going to happen. You are reliant on opportunity finding you.

Luck is about being brave and bold and striking out to do things and be things that some people might not even think you are capable of. I mean, who says you can't do that shit anyway? In fact, the more people tell you that you can't do something, that's exactly when you should think to yourself, *Just watch me!*

We need to start taking responsibility for our own lives and our own actions and begin creating our own luck. Go out, work hard, show up, be brave, be kind and luck will follow.

PART 3

EXECUTION

CHAPTER ONE

EXCUSES

WE COULD ALL COME UP WITH LIMITLESS EXCUSES AS TO why we don't fix our shit, or at least why we can't do it right now – you know, we're just waiting for that perfect moment. This is where I wish I could insert that face-slap emoji. Don't worry, I'd slap my own face first.

The truth is, you can have results or excuses, but you can't have both. We need to choose.

Here are the top three excuses I hear ALL the time:

I just don't have the time.

'I'm too busy right now. You're too busy to get your shit fixed?! Like, what else could be more important? Sleep less, wake up earlier, stop wasting time scrolling through social media, put that box set down. Get your shit fixed.

We all have twenty-four hours in a day. I promise you, you can find someone who has less available time than you do who has got their shit together. It's called prioritizing.

Please don't think I'm suggesting you have a ton of free time, I know you don't. Neither do I. So what do I do? I get up at 5.30 a.m. every single day. Could I stay in bed? Sure, but then, would have I my shit together? Probably not.

I know I'm a little weird in that I actually enjoy getting up at this time, as it sets up my day, gives me a head start and makes me feel like I own my day rather than constantly chasing my tail.

Some of you may hate this idea, and that's OK. Once you've got your shit together, you're welcome to wake up any time you like. Until then . . .

It's about structuring your time more effectively and not making excuses. Have you ever kept a time diary to see how you actually spend your time each day and how much of it you really, truly waste? Do you spend hours on Facebook, Netflix, Amazon Video? Time can literally just disappear. There is nothing wrong with any of these things, or going out with your friends, or lying in, as long as you've got your priorities right and they all come AFTER fixing your shit.

You cannot get everything done by staying in bed; it just doesn't work. Some of you might be reading this and thinking, *Ah, but I don't do any of those things*. Maybe you don't, but I guarantee that you waste just as much time doing other things. Time will run away unless you keep track of it. The reason food tracking works so well when you're dieting is that what we *think* we eat in a day and what we *really* eat in a day are often two entirely different things. Same is true for your time. How are you spending your time each day? How many times do you hit the snooze button in the morning? How long does it take you to do things? How much time do you waste because you left your keys at home, didn't charge your phone, forgot you had an appointment and had to rebook it, turned up at the wrong time . . . You get my drift.

If you don't organize your life, you might as well throw your time down a drain. The time that you put in upfront to make changes ensures you don't have to keep doing this long term. Think about where you are wasting your time right now. Stop hanging out with people who don't lift you up. Stop giving your time up to do things you don't really want to do. Stop scrolling through social media incessantly with no real purpose other than to pass the time. Start thinking about how you spend your time as closely as I hope you think about spending your money. It's a short-term sacrifice for a long-term gain.

Now is not the right time.

This is probably the worst excuse ever.

'Now isn't the right time, I'm so stressed. I've got to wait until the kids go to school. I hate my job. I'm unhappy in my relationship. I'm just so tired.' You know what? If that's how you feel, NOW is the best time ever.

If you are in a challenging situation right now, the only way to get out of it is to do something about it. It might seem counterintuitive, but this is the truth. You tell yourself now isn't the right time and you've got to wait until something else happens. And all the while you are waiting for this mythical day, your shit is getting worse.

The time when you need to be making and taking the most action is right there and then, in those moments when life is really, truly crap. So don't use the fact that life is crap as an excuse for not doing something; use it as a driver to take action and do something about it. NOW. In fact, any time you hear yourself saying, 'Now isn't the right time,' guess what? That's a clue that it is EXACTLY the right time.

Now is the only time we have. No one is guaranteed tomorrow. I know that first hand and, while I hope none of you reading this has to experience this personally, sadly, for some, it is the only wake-up call that works. Don't let that be you.

I can't do it until . . .

It's what I call the 'If, when, then' syndrome. If I do this, then I can do that. Or when I do this, then I can do that . . .

'I can't set up my new business until I've done this course. I can't start exercising until the kids have gone to school.'

'I can't sort out my relationship until I've sorted out all my other problems.'

'I can't leave the job that I hate until I've got enough money saved up.'

There's always one more obstacle, one more hurdle that you've got to overcome before you can start to face up to the things that really matter in your life. The very things that would actually fix your shit. Once. And. For. All. So stop with the hurdles. You might want to do the next course, but you don't need to wait until you've done it to start your business. You might want to lose 10lb before you join a gym, but joining the gym (and using it) will sure as hell make it easier to lose the weight. And you certainly don't need your life to be perfect before you sort your relationship out. If that was the case, none of us would ever be in a relationship.

I would urge you to take stock and ask yourself whether any of these excuses sound familiar to you? What are your go-to 'reasons' for not doing things? Maybe you could write them down, put them on the fridge or even read them out to Siri and get her to remind you of them once a week . . . Humour and sarcasm work wonders!

CHAPTER TWO

SELF-CRITICISM

MOST OF US CAN THINK BACK TO AN EARLY MEMORY OF someone saying something about us, making fun of us, maybe not even with any malice, but we took it to heart. I remember when I was about thirteen my mum saying to me, 'I wish you could be more like Katherine.' Katherine was a girl in my class and, trust me, she was nothing like me. She was calm, sedate and never raised her head above the parapet. As a parent now, I can understand why Mum might have wanted me to be more like Katherine. After all, I was mischievous, got into trouble, didn't focus very well, always wanting to get into London, ready to be an adult and do my own thing.

At first, I'll admit, it made me think, *Why aren't I good enough just as I am?* But then, the truth is, pretty quickly I started to think, *Hey, wait a minute. I don't want to be like Katherine.* I might not fit into a box, but I never smoked, drank or did drugs. I was smart, if a little challenging, and I would never give up. I liked me.

I don't know where that came from, that innate sense that I was good enough exactly as I was, but I am truly grateful for it.

There are so many negative things people tell us along the way that we have to learn to be our own champions and surround ourselves with people who will cheer us on, not drag us down.

More often than not, people really don't mean the things they say but, for most of us, they still leave a little scar. And each scar leaves a wound that needs to be healed.

Imagine positive and negative beliefs as being on a scale; you cannot control the weight of the negative beliefs that may be put on you, but you can choose whether to believe them and you can most certainly choose the positive ones you can use to outweigh them.

The problem is, the more we tell ourselves these crazy lies – that we're too young, too old, not good enough, not smart enough, not educated enough, need to be more like Katherine – well, they start to turn into beliefs.

When you're trying to break through your negative beliefs you've got to find the courage to battle through despite them. Change happens outside your comfort zone and outside your negative thoughts.

Truth is, we all have limiting beliefs. I don't think I'm a great writer; I think I'm a good writer, but I'm not going to win any literary prizes. However, I believe I am great at getting messages across that impact people's lives in a positive way, and that is far more important to me. I also think I'm pretty good at titles and cover designs . . . See: one positive belief reinforces another.

You don't have to believe that you are good at everything to believe you are good enough. If you keep telling yourself you're not good enough to get a promotion, to be in a happy relationship, to start that business idea . . . it won't happen.

But have you actually tried? I mean, *really* tried. Like, gone all in for the promotion, or been fully present in the relationship that would make you happy, or put your all into making that business idea fly?

I doubt it. You see, when people tell me they don't think they're good enough, what I see is that they start to live up to that expectation of themselves. But it's rarely based on reality. It's based on fear.

You ARE good enough.

EXERC*SE:
STOP THE SELF-CRITICISM

Let's park the things you don't like about yourself or your life for a moment. We'll come back to those. For now, I want you to do the opposite. I want you to list five things that you like about yourself or that you are proud of doing or achieving.

1.

2.

3.

4.

5.

Now I want you to talk to three of your closest friends or family members and ask them to tell you the ONE thing that they love about you the most. Write them down.

1.

2.

3.

Look at that list. Daily. No matter how much 'better' you think you could be doing right now, there are a lot of things you are doing right. There are a lot of things you've done right and will continue doing right.

Putting a halt to the self-criticism doesn't mean we become Pollyannas, believing everything we do is perfect. Far from it. We accept the things that we could do better and we work on them, but we also celebrate what we do well. What we focus on, we get more of.

CHAPTER THREE

SELF-PITY

I TOTALLY UNDERSTAND HOW HARD LIFE CAN BE. I WAS widowed in my early thirties and my life has never been the same and, just when I thought it was . . . well, it wasn't. So I get it. I really do.

But wallowing in our own misery and getting trapped in the 'poor me' syndrome is not the answer.

So what is this syndrome, and do you suffer from it? More importantly, if you do, what can you do about it?

Now before we get into this, here's a word of warning. No one likes to admit this might be them, so it's easy to dismiss the idea. Before you do that, please take a moment and ask yourself how often you find yourself in situations like this. Better to be honest and change it than sweep it under the carpet and ignore it. You don't need to make any public confessions, but a private one is a great place to start.

POOR ME . . .

* It generally develops in people who feel that life has happened *to* them; the more attention they pay to

the negative side of their life, the more they believe that story. Soon enough, it becomes a self-fulfilling prophecy.

* What starts off as a mild form of frustration or despair with their current life turns into long-term pessimism, distrust, self-pity and the belief that their life is out of their control.

* People who suffer with 'poor me' syndrome are easily spotted as they generally tend to blame other people and outside circumstances. They may not necessarily talk about it a lot, but when they do you will rarely hear them admitting they were the ones who messed things up. It will always be down to external forces and circumstances beyond their control. Either that, or it's someone else's fault.

* They seem to lurch from one drama or crisis to the next, never acknowledging the fact that they are the common denominator in creating their own crises. They often seem oblivious to reality.

* They make very little effort to learn from their mistakes or to analyse what went wrong, even though they claim to do so. The 'poor me' attitude may be a crutch, but it also creates anger, resentment and frustration in others.

* Lack of self-esteem and self-confidence typically depends on others' reactions. When others praise someone with 'poor me' syndrome, their self-esteem rises; when they're criticized, they feel worthless. In psychological terms, this is known as 'external orientation', which is not a place you want to be.

The good news is that the 'poor me' syndrome is a learned behaviour; no one is born like this. Through poor coping mechanisms and repeated habitual responses, it becomes ingrained into a person's psyche and starts to become their normality. However, it's far from normal, and it's certainly not healthy. Fortunately, you have the power to change it.

VICTIM MENTALITY

This is much more serious and, thankfully, not that common. If any of this sounds like you, I would lovingly advise speaking to a mental health practitioner.

'Victim mentality' is a psychological term that refers to a type of dysfunctional mindset whereby a person seeks out the feeling and circumstances of being 'persecuted' in order to get attention or avoid taking responsibility for themselves.

People who struggle with a victim mentality are positive that life is not only beyond their control, it is out to deliberately and specifically hurt them.

This is very destructive.

A victim is convinced that happiness can be derived only from outside of themselves and is constantly searching for external validation. If the world, the people they meet and their experiences don't make them happy, they will be unhappy. Victims truly believe they have no power to change their circumstances.

Some of the characteristic behaviours are:

* Not taking responsibility for their actions or inactions
* Wanting people to lavish them with attention
* Making people feel sorry for them by constantly talking about how hard their life is. This means

people are less likely to criticize or upset them for fear of seeming 'mean'

* Feeling they have the 'right' to complain
* Getting validation from telling people their stories
* Love of perpetual drama; it keeps them busy
* Avoidance and sidestepping of anger, and focusing instead on feeling sad

Oddly, this behaviour can make people feel quite powerful. It gives them the power and justification to avoid responsibility, the power to feel 'righteously' sad and persecuted, the power to avoid uncomfortable emotions and the power to manipulate other people.

Not only does it reward the person with a victim mentality with not having to take responsibility for their behaviour (because 'other people' are always responsible), it also prevents them from feeling uncomfortable emotions like guilt and anger, while at the same time making them feel 'cared for' by others.

Such people rarely see the impact this behaviour has on those around them. Accepting that you will never be able to please a victim becomes very common among both loved ones and work colleagues.

While I'm no therapist (and, as I said, I strongly recommend you see one if you feel you are exhibiting any of these behaviours), there are some simple tips to address this way of thinking.

1.
REPLACE 'YOU' WITH 'I'

This can help teach people to take more responsibility for their own happiness. It also helps with communication with others. Instead of saying, 'You made me mad,' say, 'I feel angry when you behave like that.'

2.
SWITCH FROM VICTIM TO SURVIVOR

A victim fights against life; a survivor embraces it.
A victim lives in the past; a survivor lives in the present.
A victim believes they're helpless; a survivor takes back control.
Note: Although the victim mentality is addictive, the survivor mentality is much more empowering in the long run.

3.
DON'T BEAT YOURSELF UP

Victim mentality is a trained behaviour, so the more gentle you can be with yourself as you learn to untangle it and get help, the easier it will be to change.

4.
TAKE RESPONSIBILITY

Start to notice all the ways you shy away from responsibility. This can be hard to look at and accept, but be honest with yourself. Think about how gaining sympathy from other people made you feel special, wanted or loved, and how it makes the cycle of blaming others continue.

5.
SERVICE TO OTHERS

When we play the victim, we tend to be focused on ourselves. It's time to get yourself out of your head by doing something for someone else. Realizing that you can feel good without manipulating another person is a great way to curb the victim mentality.

EXERC*SE:
STOP THE SELF-PITY

Trust me, the 'poor me' syndrome might feel good temporarily, but it is the very worst thing you can do if you want to fix your shit.

We all go through times when we feel the world is against us. Let's be honest, we all go through times when we are *sure* the world is against us. Everything that could go wrong does go wrong, and it seems relentless.

It's OK during these times to feel sorry for ourselves; it's human nature. We *all* do it, myself included. The problem is, when we stay stuck feeling like this for prolonged periods of time, our perception becomes our reality.

Stop for a second and ask yourself, how are these feelings serving you? Are they helping you? Are they lifting you out of the ditch or digging you deeper?

The trick when we get stuck in this rut is to use these feelings as an engine, not a brake. Turn them into a strength. I know this sounds and probably feels counterintuitive, but it's like rocket fuel when you get it right.

Imagine every little shitty thing that's happened to you, everything that's been going wrong, and picture it as fuel for your fire. Turn every negative thing into a strength. Use it to drive you forward.

One sure-fire way of dealing with self-pity is to replace it with gratitude. When you are in the midst of feeling like life is against you, it's hard to feel grateful for anything. Yet this is exactly the time that you need to remind yourself of all the things you have to be grateful for. Even if they seem like very small things!

You can start by writing down three things that you have to be grateful for in life – it might be your dog, your best friend, your partner, your health, the fact that it's a sunny day ... Often, remembering the beauty in the simplest things, the things that we mostly take for granted, reminds us that life isn't so bad after all.

CHAPTER FOUR

GETTING HUNG UP
ON MISTAKES

JUST BECAUSE YOU MESSED UP YESTERDAY DOESN'T MEAN
you're going to do the same thing today. But remember: good
intentions by themselves are hollow victories; they're a pla-
cebo effect with no real impact. Only action works.

Started a diet but already back to eating doughnuts? Stop.
Put the book down, go and get a rubbish bag and go to your
kitchen. Throw out everything that isn't good for you. The bis-
cuits, the sugar, the bread, the white rice (white anything), the
alcohol, the ready-made meals, the mayonnaise, the coleslaw,
anything with sugar in it, the crisps, the snacks . . . all of it. Yep,
I'm for real. Do it now. Got nothing left in your cupboards?
Good, that's a great place to start. Go food shopping and don't
go buying any more of that shit. Time to get real about making
a change.

Messed up a presentation at work or lost a client? Go out
and work twice as hard next time. Don't let it send you in a
downward spiral. We all mess up some things. I've lost lots of
client pitches over the years, often for reasons beyond my control, but I tried to learn from every experience to give myself a

better chance of success the next time. No one likes making mistakes but, as trite as it can sound, we can learn from every mistake we make – if we're open to it.

You start to make progress, but then you slip up. You start beating yourself up and, rather than accepting it for what it is, a mistake or a bad decision, and learning from it, it becomes like a game of snakes and ladders. You're so close to making real change and, just as you're nearly there, you make a mistake and end up twenty places behind. This not only sets you back, but it gets you thinking that it's just not going to work for you like it does for other people, and you spiral. You run. You bury your head in the sand. At the very time you should stand upright, breathe and face the challenge head on, you do the opposite. You hide and hand the mistake the power to take away what you really want. If instead you stood up, looked that mistake in the eye and learned from it, you could move forward. So this time, choose differently. This time, change the outcome.

Remember, so much of this is in your head. Stop beating yourself up over it. Just own up to the situation and rectify it. Then move on.

If people hold grudges against you for your mistakes, they are not people worth having in your life. Depending on how grave the mistake was, it might take even the most forgiving person some time to truly mend. However, it is down to you and it is in YOUR control to make the healing process quicker; for you and for them. Instead of running away and pretending things haven't happened, talk, be honest, be vulnerable.

The people who love you, love you despite the mistakes you make. The people who don't, well, they're the ones who hold grudges to use as leverage against you. Understand the difference between the two and treat them accordingly.

Now that doesn't mean you should go taking those who love you for granted, thinking that they know you didn't mean it, or that because they love you, you don't need to talk about it. You do, it's part of your growth and their healing. They won't throw it back in your face, you'll just make them feel loved and you'll make yourself feel proud.

And when you do, you'll realize you make far fewer mistakes, because you are no longer so scared of screwing up that it becomes a self-fulfilling prophecy.

You've always known what the right thing to do is, and now is the time to start doing it.

EXERC*SE:
STOP GETTING HUNG UP ON MISTAKES

We all make mistakes, but remember: your past does not equal your future. In fact, we learn the most from our mistakes because, every time something doesn't work out, we are one step closer to ensuring the next time it does.

Let's put that to the test ... Write down your three biggest mistakes. It could be in your business, in your personal life, your career, your friendships ... anything.

Now write down three things that you have learned from each of these mistakes.

You see, these are life lessons, not mistakes.

I remember, when I first started out in business, I made some grave mistakes. Once, I lost £10,000 in a really stupid decision. It nearly sank my business, but it also taught me a very valuable lesson. When I looked at it in the cold light of day, I realized that if that mistake had happened later on, it could have cost me £100,000.

I choose to remind myself of all the things that I get right, the things that I'm good at, and try to become better at them. I'm not foolish enough not to recognize my mistakes, but I don't dwell on them. I accept them fully, learn my lesson and move forward.

There is no shame in making mistakes.
No one learned to ride a bike without first falling off.

CHAPTER FIVE

SELF-SABOTAGE

DO YOU LEARN FROM YOUR MISTAKES OR KEEP REPEAT-ing them? Do you tell yourself that when x has happened, then you'll be able to fix your shit? But somehow, x never happens, or, if it does, y simply takes its place.

Maybe what you're really doing is creating excuses for not moving forward or making a change. A way out from facing up to the reality that your life isn't where you want it to be?

Tip: If you keep doing this, it never will be.

CHAPTER SIX

WORRYING BEFORE
IT'S EVEN HAPPENED

SOME PEOPLE ARE AFRAID OF REJECTION, SOME ARE AFRAID of letting other people down, some are afraid of success, of failure, of not being perfect. Some people don't even know what they are afraid of, they just feel this fear taking hold.

Until you make a decision that you're going to do something about it, nothing is going to change. But the moment you understand what you are afraid of, you have to ask yourself a very important question. Is it REAL?

Ninety-nine per cent of the time, it won't be . . . or, at least, you think it's a lion when really it's a cat. Most of our fears are in our heads. We tend to perpetuate the worst-case scenario, playing out these roles in our head, subconsciously, and sometimes consciously, too. We keep thinking that the worst thing that could possibly happen is actually going to happen. We start to believe that the worst thought we are harbouring in our head is real, but it's not. The things you think about, the things you think are going to happen, are actually very, very unlikely to.

You have to get logical about this, and the way you do that

is by taking back control and acknowledging that you feel really scared about this particular situation but that it is a feeling and not necessarily a reality. It's far better to acknowledge that you feel scared and then do something about it.

EXERC*SE:
THE WORST-CASE SCENARIO

When faced with trying something new, making a change or radically altering your life, we think about all the variables: what could go right and, of course, what could go wrong.

Our first thoughts typically jump to the worst-case scenario. What is the absolute worst thing that could happen if we go down this path? Our minds get stuck here, in quicksand. We can't move.

Some people would advise you against focusing on your worst-case scenario, as it quite often puts you off the very thing you are wanting to do. However, I have a different view. I think we should face our worst-case scenarios head on, look at them in the cold light of day and ask ourselves, is this really ever going to happen?

I remember talking to a woman who wanted to start her own business. She was a doctor but had always wanted to be in business. She had so many great ideas but had not pursued even one of them. When I asked her why, her reasons astounded me. She had played out the worst-case scenario so many times it had become reality. So we unpacked it . . .

What is the worst that could happen?

'It could all go wrong and I'd lose all my money.'

OK, and if that did happen (which was entirely unlikely), what would happen then?

'I'd lose my home because I wouldn't have any money to pay the mortgage.'

Wow. She had gone from being in a highly paid job as a doctor to being homeless in the space of sixty seconds.

I asked her how much she earned in her current job. She said, '£80,000 a year.' I asked her if it had been hard to find her job. She said, 'Not at all, there is a very big shortage of doctors, especially in London.' I asked her how much her mortgage was. She said, 'Twelve hundred pounds a month,' and I asked, 'So would it be fair to say that you need about £3,000 a month to cover all your expenses and have a little left over?' She replied, 'Yes, or maybe even a bit less.'

I asked her one last question.

'How long does it take for a doctor to find a new job right now?'

'Oh, about a month. But if you don't mind where you work, you can find something the next day.'

I looked at her calmly . . .

'So the worst-case scenario really is that your business doesn't work out and that you go back and get a highly paid job doing exactly what you're doing now.'

The penny dropped.

Now it's your turn.

Write down something you want to do that you haven't done. Something you are scared of doing. Think about what's held you back.

Now write down what the very worst thing is that could happen if you were to pursue this goal.

Look at it in black and white and ask yourself, how likely is it that this will really happen? Mark it on a scale of 1 to 10. Anything less than 6, you are going to totally ignore and simply move forward.

Now look at that scenario again and ask yourself, if this were to happen, what could you do? Write down three courses of action. Now write down what help you would need and from whom. Create a plan to deal with your worst-case scenario and, immediately, it will seem like a molehill rather than a mountain.

When you face your worst-case scenario head on, it slowly starts to diminish.

CHAPTER SEVEN
LISTENING TO
YOUR INSTINCT

YOUR INSTINCT TELLS YOU TO DO THE RIGHT THING, BUT years of conditioning can make us view change as something to be afraid of, so instead your defence mechanism jumps in and sends you back down another dead end. Why? Because it feels comfortable.

Whether it's your eating habits, your relationships or your work, your instinct tells you the right thing to do and your habits sabotage it.

Then you feel guilty. And the cycle keeps repeating itself.

Until you learn to break it.

You have to learn to listen to your instinct and follow it *immediately*, before your negative muscle memory has a chance to derail it.

The moment you try to make a change, to do something differently, you will start to feel uncomfortable and scared. Then, that good ol' monkey brain of yours will chime in with all the reasons why this is a *bad* idea . . . This is a sign that you are doing the right thing! Follow it. Listen to it.

EXERC*SE:
START LISTENING TO YOUR INSTINCT

Your instinct isn't some 'woo woo' radar. It's the summation of all your years of experience coming together in that one second to give you instant feedback on how you should handle a particular situation. I think of it as *The Matrix* meets *Limitless* (if you haven't watched these films, they're a great way to spend a Sunday evening).

Some psychologists, most famously Carl Jung, have theorized that we are born with the memories and experiences of our ancestors imprinted on our DNA. We're not necessarily unlocking them, but it's possible that our most basic survival instincts might stem from some trauma experienced many years ago, not even in our own lifetimes.

So how do you start to tap into your instinct more?

Have you ever felt as though something was not right, or felt a certain way about a situation? Maybe you felt unsafe at a particular moment, or uneasy around someone?

This isn't just a random feeling, this is your instinct, your intuition – otherwise known as a 'gut' feeling.

Being able to trust your gut and your intuition is powerful, and even more so when you can really understand the signs your intuition is trying to give you. But how do you develop your intuition? Better still, how can you learn to trust your instinct?

Here are five simple ways to help you do just that.

1. Listen to it. It's like a muscle: the more you use it, the stronger it gets.

2. Meditate. Truth is, this is hard for me, but find your own way of mediating (I run) and you will find it easier to tap into your instinct.

3. Live life in the present. Stop worrying about the past or the future and focus on the moment.

4. Observe your energy levels around different people and environments. This is your gut feeling advising you on what is good for you and what is not.

5. Write a diary. Don't bury your feelings, track them. If you start to see patterns arising around particular people or situations, then that is likely to be your instinct trying to tell you something.

CHAPTER EIGHT

TRYING NEW THINGS

BY NOT DOING ANYTHING DIFFERENTLY, BY NOT CHAN-
ging your tactics or your habits, you are 100 per cent going to
fail because, if it was working, it would be working right now.

I would be so bold as to say, if you're not doing something
every day to move you closer to the goal of what you really
want, you are already failing. You are currently sabotaging your
own success. You are sabotaging the very things that you want
in your life, and what for? You are undoubtedly afraid of something, so the first step is to figure out what that is so you can
overcome it.

EXERC*SE:
START TRYING NEW THINGS

A lot of us stay stuck in the same routines and comfort zones because, frankly, it can be scary doing
something new. However, how are we to grow our

businesses, our relationships and ourselves if we constantly do the same things over and over again?

Most of the time we don't try new things because of what 'might' happen . . . We make up scenarios and results that we don't know to be true (and most of the time are far from true) so we stay doing the same old things.

Trying new things can open up such huge possibilities. By trying new things we come into contact with new experiences, people, ideas, cultures . . . the list is endless. It's a constant education that we can learn from, choosing what will help us to get to where we want to be and ignoring what doesn't. When it's put like that, what's not to love about seeking out new things!

So I challenge you to try the things below. What have you got to lose?

Try:

One new food
One new activity
One new place
One new book
One new movie
One new person

And why not create a bucket list, a list of things you want to do and places you want to go before you die, and then start ticking them off?

CHAPTER NINE
TAKING RESPONSIBILITY

YOU WILL NEVER FIX ANYTHING BY RUNNING FROM LIFE. Or from reality. If you keep on doing what you've always done, you're going to stay exactly where you are.

But please be clear, your reality right now does NOT define you, it simply gives you the current truth to work with. This is often the hardest step to take, but it's also crucial. That, reaching out for help and, of course, taking action will be the catalyst you need.

One of my biggest frustrations is when people nod their head in agreement with you, tell you they're going to change and then do absolutely nothing about it. Nothing.

I realize that sometimes this is a protection mechanism, guarding against much bigger problems. Sometimes people are literally scared stiff to reach out for help. I'm hoping reading this book will be a start.

We are not supposed to have all the answers - no one can - but, together, we can find them.

In the words of one of my favourite poets, John Donne, 'No man is an island entire of itself.'

So many people become disconnected from their life, their challenges, even their dreams. It's as if their life is no longer their own, as if they are simply looking on from the outside. In extreme cases, they start to justify in their own minds that nothing can be done because it all feels as if it is happening to someone else. And when it feels like it's happening to someone else, you start to act like it's happening to someone else. You divest responsibility for your life on to someone else, to your circumstances, to your environment, to your problems. You give up.

That needs to stop right now; it's time to man up and fix your shit. And for clarity, in this instance, 'man up' is not gender-specific. Not that I thought you were going to get all PC on me, but you know, just in case!

The most important thing you can do when fixing your shit is to actually DO it. Not just talk about doing it.

You're not lazy, you're just stuck in a rut and don't know how to get out. When all you've been taught is how to dig . . . Well, no wonder the rut is just getting deeper. It's time to learn to build ladders. The things you need to get out.

Just because you're doing something one way doesn't mean it's going to get you where you want to go. In fact, it's pretty certain that, if it were, you'd already be there.

However, in order to make that change, you have to really *want* to, not merely *prefer* to.

We need to take personal responsibility for our own thoughts and actions. How we treat other people has an impact on both us and them and, of course, sometimes we make mistakes, and that is when we need to grow up and own them. If you don't own them, you can't fix them. That is growth.

Sometimes people can mistakenly think that taking responsibility will just make things worse, yet the fact is, it makes things better. Responsibility and structure lead to better habits, and better habits lead to less stress, and less stress leads to a better life.

You want to go for a promotion but instead you just keep

things ticking over, trying to make ends meet at the end of each month. A promotion would mean more work and maybe some studying, and that just seems like more than you can handle right now. Wrong. It's exactly what you need right now. A constructive focus.

You might do the same with relationships, for fear that you're just going to keep on messing things up, but that's not the case. Yesterday is not today, and today is not tomorrow.

Rome wasn't built in a day, it was built day by day.

If you're constantly talking about wanting to make differences to your life, to improve your fitness, to stop smoking, to set up your own business, to put things right . . . but you never actually do it, well, you're going to regret that shit for life.

EXERC*SE:
START TAKING RESPONSIBILITY

This is an exercise I do with my clients, my friends and for myself on a regular basis.

It starts by looking at the reality of your stresses, challenges and problems in the cold light of day rather than as the jumbled mess they might currently be occupying in your head.

Take out a sheet of paper and write down three columns:

Column 1: Write down the things that are stressing you out right now.

Column 2: Write down the solution. You might not have the solution at your fingertips, but write down what it would be if you did.

Column 3: Write down what needs to happen for what's in column 2 to be able to happen.

What's stressing you out?

PROBLEM	SOLUTION	WHAT I NEED TO DO
① I don't like my job.	Find a job you love or start your own business.	• Upskill – Update your CV – Apply for a new job – Start your own business.
② I'm overweight.	Lose weight. Get fit.	• Get clear on how much weight you need to lose – Throw away all your junk food – Create a schedule for the gym – Food diary.
③ I want to give up smoking.	Give up.	• Create a plan – Patches – What else could you do with the money?
④ I'm in debt.	Clear your debt. Earn more money.	• How much debt do you have? Get clear – Switch to lower-rate cards - Rent out your spare bedroom.
⑤ I'm not happy.	Figure out what makes you happy.	• List five things you love but have stopped doing.
⑥ I'm not in a great relationship.	Get into one.	• Start with some tough love – Get out – Create a great relationship with yourself first.

CHAPTER TEN

CREATING HOPE

IN THAT VERY MOMENT THAT YOU MAKE A DECISION TO do something about it, something incredible happens: you create hope.

Hope is something that drives us forward, hope is the fuel for taking action, hope is the thing that gets us from here to there. When you make a decision to take action, hope pops up even when you didn't feel like it was there two seconds before. Why? Because taking action gives you your power back. You get control back the moment you say, 'Right, I'm done. I'm going to do something about it.' In that moment, when you have hope, you've also got the power and the courage to change, because that's what happens when you make a decision. That is the time to take action. Do not let hope dissipate. Act on it.

The trick is to act on it straight away. Don't let that monkey brain take over. You know, the one with all the negative chatter. It doesn't matter how big or small the action is - it might be as simple as sending a text or registering a domain name for a new business idea - but it's something that takes you closer to where you want to be rather than further away. Every day you let slip by between you and your goal, you're just building a bigger and bigger wall to climb over to reach it.

When we're scared to take action what happens is we let another day pass, and another day, and then another . . . and now it seems like the gulf between where we are and where we want to be is getting wider and wider. Like when you don't go to the gym. The first day off? Just a day. The second day, no problem. But before you know it, it's three weeks and, all of a sudden, it's hard to get back into your routine.

The same is true if you've ever had an argument with someone. You think to yourself, *You know what, I just want to make up.* It doesn't really matter who is right or who is wrong, I just want to reach out. But then what happens is another day goes past, and then three months have gone and you're thinking, *Wow, now it's too late.*

It is NEVER too late. Not that you should let three months pass - you shouldn't - but don't let the mistakes of the past become the mistakes of the future.

EXERC*SE:
START CREATING HOPE

We've all heard of the act of paying it forward, and this is where I believe we can create hope in our lives. It's the small things that make the biggest differences to people. When someone notices something about you that you thought was hidden, or something you said months ago and they remembered, or they know just the right thing to say at the right time, it can make you feel amazing. It's also amazing to be the person who does that for other people. To see what joy you can bring to others, just by showing them you see them.

I'm a BIG believer in karma and that what you put out in the world will come right back at you, tenfold. When you give others a little bit of hope, you set up a boomerang for it to return to you. You will start to trust that everything will work out and that the changes you are making will be impactful.

In this exercise, I want you to do five things for others. They don't have to be big things. It can be as simple as texting that person you've not seen in ages to say hi. Book something they've always wanted to do. Send them something in the post. I've given you three examples to help you on your way. Now it's your turn.

1.
2.
3.
4.
5.

CHAPTER ELEVEN
ASKING FOR HELP

SOMETIMES, THE HARDEST THING TO DO IS TO ASK FOR help. But if, say, you're drinking every day of the week, chances are the problem is far more serious. If your work or personal life has been affected by your drinking, it's time to get help. There are many ways to do this: sign up to Alcoholics Anonymous and commit to the Twelve-step Programme. Tell people close to you what you are doing so they can support you. An alcoholic isn't someone who needs to limit their drinking, they are someone who needs to never touch alcohol again. And to do this requires help, even for the strongest of us. Put the book down, pick up the phone and make the call. Get help.

Asking for help applies to everything. Need help writing your CV? Ask for it. Need help with figuring out your next career move? Ask for it.

Society has led us to believe that asking for help is a sign of weakness, but it is the greatest sign of strength.

It's time to dispel this myth, once and for all.

A 2017 study in the *Journal of Health Psychology* examined factors that prevented men who were suffering from depression from seeking help. Some of the reasons they gave were:

People will think less of me for needing help.

I should be able to fix this myself.

I want to fix this myself.

I wouldn't know what sort of help is available.

I'm ashamed I can't fix it.

I don't like to talk about my feelings.

While this study was specifically looking at the reasons men with depression struggle to seek help, the truth is that many, if not all, of these reasons apply to other situations and, of course, to women, too.

People are afraid that asking for help, whether in their business or in their personal life, will make them seem weak. Fear, pride and ego stand in the way of solving problems more quickly and with far less pain.

The truth is, it takes courage to ask for help. What if people say no? What if they think I'm weak?

What if they don't? What if you could fix your shit so much quicker with a little helping hand?

Sometimes it's the big things, like depression, losing your job, a failed relationship, but sometimes it's as simple as asking someone to pick you up from the airport or watch the kids.

We hate the idea of seeming like we haven't got it all together (although we don't actually know anyone who does) and we hate the thought that people might let us down. So we struggle on in silence.

How easily we forget that we all have issues and that we all need help. Every single one of us.

So switch perspectives and start thinking about the role that you have to play in other people's successes. If you shut them out from helping you, you don't leave the door open for them to ask for help when they need it.

Think you have nothing to bring to the table? Think again. We all have different skills and strengths and we all need different types of support. Sometimes, just showing up is all you need to do for someone.

Let's get one thing clear: by pretending everything is OK when it's not, you're not being strong, you're being foolish. You're just acting tough. Masking your pain and hiding your problems won't make anything better. It makes things worse.

Running and hiding never solve anything.

Asking for help, however, does; it makes things better and it makes you stronger. It means you are strong enough to admit that you don't have all the answers. None of us does.

Asking for and accepting help means you are facing your challenges head on and are willing to be vulnerable. You've got to be prepared not just to ask for help but also to accept it. If people are willing to give it to you, you've got to be ready to accept it. When things go wrong in our lives, we all need a helping hand. We all need somebody to pull us up. I can't tell you how many times people have pulled me up, and I can't tell you how many times I've probably been dragged up when I didn't even want to be. So I'm grateful to the people in my life who have pulled me up, who show up for me and are by my side when I'm faltering. I am also grateful for the opportunity to help pull others up, too.

So whatever it is you are struggling with, it starts with being honest, with yourself and with others. By letting people in, people who care about you and want to help you, your shit will get fixed a lot more quickly.

Sometimes people think that staying away from others when they're not feeling their best is protecting them from their shit, but that depends on who the people are. Personally, I'm like a tardigrade (ha, bet you'd never heard that one before!), also known as a water bear. It's a microscopic critter that can withstand just about anything, including a nuclear explosion. So, before you make decisions for other people, have an honest conversation with them.

Sure, I get it you don't want the added stress of people worrying about you on top of your own worries, or to worry about the impact you're having on someone else's life. So don't. And no, it's really not easier said than done. It's easier done. You'd be amazed how quickly problems can be resolved when you really want to fix them and are prepared not just to ask for and accept help but also be open to doing things differently. If what you're doing isn't working, there's a lesson in that. It's time to change what you're doing and how you are doing it.

Can you imagine Chewbacca telling Han Solo, 'Sorry, dude, that's past my stress threshold'? Or Batman saying to Robin, 'Sorry, mate, I'm only here for the good times'? Hell, no. They are the Dynamic Duo! And one thing I know for sure, Bonnie wouldn't tell Clyde she couldn't handle it. They're a team. So they fight it together. Got it?

Asking for help is like a muscle: the more you use it, the stronger and easier it gets. The more support you get, the less you will need it going forward, because in the process you will become better equipped to deal with future challenges.

It is a sad irony that, at the times we need help the most, we are least likely to ask for it. Sometimes, you've just got to take a leap of faith.

By not asking for help, not only are you struggling when you don't need to, you are also depriving those who love you of the opportunity to be there for you. And if you don't accept their help and support, they are far less likely to ask for yours. Everyone loses.

We all have gifts to share; what is easy for one may be hard for another. That's the beauty of life. We can all do so much more together than we can alone.

The answer isn't to tough it out, it's to reach out.

EXERC*SE:
START ASKING FOR HELP

Asking for help is something most people find really challenging. Even if people say to us, 'If there's any-thing I can do to help, just let me know,' we smile, say thank you and then ignore it or don't follow up. In my experience, if people offer help, they mean it! So why do we find it so difficult to ask for help? Mostly because we don't want to look vulnerable, or stupid, or both.

For this exercise, I want you to write out a list of everything you currently feel you need help with. Then, in a separate list, write down the names of the people who have offered you their help over the years. Looking at both lists, match them up, so you have a person next to what you need help with.

Now the hard part . . . Pick one from the list and reach out to that person and ask them to help you with the thing you put their name against. Be spe-cific. 'I know you offered to help me if I needed it and I could really do with your help this Friday to go through my CV.' A simple example, but it's very clear what you need help with.

PART 4

YOUR SH*T TO FIX

CHAPTER ONE

LIFE SH*T

LITTLE BOMBS

We're going to have little bombs going off all the time, literally every single week, and maybe, on a bad week, every single day.

I remember a while ago I was running a two-day workshop that people had paid a lot of money to attend, and we were also filming it for those who couldn't attend. Now, I'm not going to pretend that I am ultra-glamorous all the time, I'm not, but I do like to put a little bit of effort into looking polished for events and filming. There is also the very important point that I am incapable of blow-drying my own hair. The one time I made an attempt to use a curling wand, I ended up looking like Harry Potter, with a lightning scar in the middle of my forehead. There is a reason my motto in life is:

Tie your hair up in a ponytail, put on some gangsta rap, drink a cup of coffee and handle it.

I can't do anything else with my hair!

So I'm sitting in the hotel waiting for my make-up artist (who also does my hair) and she's still not there. Now, she is usually super-early, so I'm beginning to wonder what is going on. Turns out she's in Southampton, which is about four hours away from where I was, in London! She had mixed the dates up. So here I am, in central London, not even at my own house, with no hair dryer and no make-up. And most of the shops don't open until 9 a.m. My event starts at 9 a.m.

I quickly google twenty-four-hour chemists and find one not too far away. I run in and grab whatever I can . . . a hairbrush is always a good start, some make-up (pretty sure I never used it again) and some hair bands. Yep, you guessed it, I put my hair up in a ponytail and handled it.

Yes, I know that this really was a First World problem and a very little bomb, but it's how we react to the day-to-day stuff that has a bigger impact on the big stuff.

What was the option? Let it impact my day? Hell, no. As I said, it was a First World problem. I mean, c'mon, 'Hell, I have no make-up artist!' OK, not having any make-up or a hair dryer was a little more of a problem but, like most things, you can find a solution with a little bit of ingenuity. Even if it's not an ideal one.

When things start to go wrong, it is easy to fall into the snow-ball effect. We start to think that the next thing is going to go wrong, that the whole day is going to go wrong. So stop and take stock. What is within your control to fix right now? Fix it. How much of this situation are you in control of? What are you doing to fix it? I know my example might seem trivial, especially to the guys reading this who are probably thinking, *Why were you even worried about that at all?!* But that's kinda my point. It's amazing how small some of the things we let affect us really are.

The first thing you can take control of is your own state of mind. We can all influence how we interpret situations. My make-up artist made a mistake. What was I going to do? Get pissed off with her? It's not as if I have never made any mistakes! I just made the best I could of the situation in hand. I got myself back into control of the situation by grabbing a hair-brush, some mascara and some hair bands. Yep, I know, I wish all our problems were this easily fixed, too, but the principle is the same. Take control before things spiral out of control . . . and usually, that happens in your own mind before the reality happens.

Focus on the good things . . . like the fact that we had a great event, with great content and great delegates. It even gave me a great topic for social media later that day . . .

If your relationship is heading for the rocks, step in and do something about it before it crashes. If your business isn't really working the way you want it to, or maybe you've just lost a client, don't go burying your head in the sand. Of course, I've been guilty of this at points in my life, too. Thinking that somehow, miraculously, when I pull my head out, everything will have been sorted. How was that going to happen? I had no idea.

When we run away, we give control to the situation. If you want to deal with something when it's going wrong, you have to take back control. So you've lost a client, what are you going to do about it? You can try to win them back. That usually doesn't work. So what can you do, then? Firstly, figure out how much money this is going to mean losing. What is the bottom line to your business? Usually when you lose a client, they have to give you notice so you don't lose the income straight away. Usually, you'll have at least three months, depending on the terms of your contract. (Note: if you don't have at least three months' notice written into your contracts, please go and update them now!)

So you lose the client, but you've still got the money coming in for a few more months. You know what happens with most people? Somehow, our brains turn to mush and we don't do anything. We are paralysed by fear. We resort to wishful thinking: *Something will happen . . . something will come up . . .* Well, my friend, wishful thinking rarely works.

When shit goes wrong, you've got to do something about it. Don't panic. Act. How are you going to make up that income? Instead of pretending it hasn't happened, get out there and be proactive. You've got to do whatever you need to do to get that income back in. What can happen if you're not careful is that you get caught in the trial of feeling sorry for yourself and blaming other people. The thing is, it doesn't really matter whose fault it is, what matters is fixing it. Don't let the situation take you down.

Last year, my car was written off when a tree from the park I live opposite crashed through a wall and literally smashed it in half. My car was the only one on the road. Only one tree fell down . . . and it's a big park with a lot of trees. Now I'll admit, I did get a little *Why did this have to happen to me?!* Especially when the car had come back the night before from the garage and had had a full service, new tyres fitted – the whole nine yards. Now add to that the fact that I didn't even park my car there (I have a driveway), but the guy from the garage did, and I really could have started thinking the universe was conspiring against me.

The reality was it was insured. No one was hurt. The park is a royal park, and there was zero dispute, they paid all my excess and my hire-car costs. The bonus . . . a brand-new car. Every cloud, and all that.

If that wasn't enough, within the space of two weeks I found myself lying face up in the very same park looking up at the sky. I had gone for a run. It was a beautiful Saturday morning, the sun was shining and I didn't need any convincing to get out the door. I got about a mile and a half, through the rose gardens, around the trees . . . and then I'm not entirely sure what happened. I just remember looking at the sky and there being three worried faces looking down on me. Turns out I had been knocked out . . . by a Labrador.

One woman was on the phone to the ambulance, another was apologizing, tears streaming down her cheeks, and then I felt something wet: a black Labrador was licking my face. I thought I was dreaming, but then I felt the pain in my head and my leg. The woman on the phone was describing what had happened. Apparently, the dog had come out of nowhere, chasing a squirrel, and had run straight into me. It was like a rugby tackle. I was thrown in the air and landed on my back, concussed. My usual run ended up in a trip to A&E in an ambulance.

Luckily, apart from the mass bruising, I was OK, but it crossed my mind more than once: what if it had been a car? How can we ever see these things coming?

The truth is that, while we can try to prevent life from blindsiding us, sometimes it really is out of our control. So what do we do when life throws us a curveball? First, take a gratitude stockcheck. For me, I knew that my friend Denise was making sure someone was there to look after my son, Jett, and was also checking on me. I was grateful that it was a dog and not a car and that I lived to tell the tale. Being knocked out by a Labrador was not the way I had planned to go.

Next, take stock of your life. Do you have a will? If you couldn't earn any money for three months, what would happen? Do you have savings? Who would look after you? Are you prepared?

These moments in life, the ones when everything feels out of control, are also the times when you can find the greatest clarity. You see the people who are really there for you. The ones who make the effort: show up, come round – be there.

When the breath is literally knocked out of you, see it as an opportunity to step back and reassess. Are you doing the right things, with the right people? Are your time, energy and love focused on the things that truly matter? Are there conversations left unsaid? What do you want to do differently? If it all ended tomorrow, would your life have been well lived? I hope so. If not, it's time to start living.

BIG BOMBS

These are the life-altering, earth-shattering events that we all wish no one ever had to go through. I'm hoping none of these will ever affect you but, if they do, I would like to at least give you a heads-up on handling them as best you can. Some people come through these types of situations stronger than before and others struggle to recover. I want to help make sure you're the former.

CRITICAL ILLNESS

If you have been diagnosed with a long-term or critical illness, your world will have been shaken to the core. You will have so many questions, not just about what happens next, but why you, why this and why now? That's before you start to think of all the practicalities of making sure your loved ones are taken care of or how you are going to adjust to living with a long-term illness.

There is no easy answer, nor is there a one-size-fits-all solution. Whether the illness is physical or mental, you will need support, and the sooner you start asking for it, the better.

If you're reading this and you are in fine shape, then I would urge you to use this as a wake-up call to a) get full critical-illness cover (if you can afford it, and if you can't, go and read the chapter on money) and b) book yourself in for a full body MOT. It will be the best few hundred pounds that you could spend.

MENTAL HEALTH

I am entirely ill equipped to give any seasoned advice on dealing with this silent epidemic, other than to say, you are not alone. It breaks my heart to know how many people I have close to me, people who I love and care about, who are suffering right now as I write this yet still feel too stigmatized to reach out and ask for help.

Yes, the world is changing, but it is doing so very slowly.

> One in every six adults has mental health issues. One in every hundred has serious mental health issues. (Nuffield Trust, 2015)

> Three in every four UK suicides are male. (CALM, 2018)

> One in eight children and young people aged between five and nineteen has a mental disorder. (NHS, 2017)

Mental health is being talked about more and more, and I truly hope these numbers start to go down. Please don't suffer in silence. Reach out to CALM, Mind, the Samaritans and your friends . . . Don't suffer alone.

DIVORCE

Now I need to make a caveat here: I have never been divorced – in fact, I've never been married (not against it, just hasn't happened) – but I will say that I am proud and grateful that I am still friends with every guy I've had a significant relationship with since I was sixteen. I've always believed that, if you choose a good person from the beginning, then even if it doesn't work out, they should still be a good person in the end. Truth is, we all change as we grow into ourselves and relationships fall apart for all kinds of reasons. Sometimes, it's just so that you can find the person you are truly meant to be with and, yes, I do realize that sounds just a little 'woo woo'. Mostly, though, relationships fail because you are growing in different directions. Staying with someone through guilt or obligation is a recipe for disaster.

While I have not been through a divorce myself, I have lived through my parents getting divorced, which was horrific and left us destitute. I've also been on the sidelines as more than a couple of my friends have gone through the same process, with varying degrees of trauma. One thing to accept is that you can never, ever change anyone other than yourself. This is crucial to remember during any break-up, whether it's a romantic relationship or a business one.

Ultimately, your only goal is to be the best person you can be during the process without being walked all over. If the other party acts like a bully, then you need to put Mr Nice Guy aside and bring out the lawyers. There is no point pretending you are going to sort this out amicably if you know you are not. Running and hiding won't help either.

Try, where possible, to keep emotions out of it; just focus on the facts and, if you have children, they need to be your number-one priority over everything, including money.

Like everything else in life, the better your communication through the process, the better the outcome for everyone. If you can't communicate, accept that early on and go through lawyers. I don't believe in trying to make a silk purse out of a sow's ear. Neither do I believe in creating unnecessary drama. So it is a balance. Be kind, but don't be weak. Put the children first. Money second. Keep personal vendettas out of it, no matter how justified they might feel. The best revenge, should you feel you need it, is you being happy.

LOSS

Sadly, I have no caveats here. I am far too fully equipped to comment. I wish I wasn't.

In my mid-thirties I was knocked out by possibly the largest curveball that life could throw at me: my best friend, my partner and my son's dad, passed away, leaving me totally bereft in every way imaginable. It felt like I had lost three people close to me by losing him.

Even now, years later, I find it hard to fully explain the pain such a loss causes. I can't sugarcoat it. It doesn't get easier – this is an old wives' tale that people tell in the hope of making someone feel better in the moment. The real truth is that life is different afterwards. The pain subsides but, like a scar, it's always there. It becomes woven into the tapestry of our lives and, hopefully, we find a way for it to shape our future that leaves a legacy for those no longer here.

When you lose someone close to you, especially unexpectedly, I think most of us go through PTSD to one degree or another. It can take years to recover from the shock. For me, I have no real memories of the first two years after Steve's death. I remember nothing. It was like I was anaesthetized the whole time, wandering around in a stupor, my feelings paralysed by loss.

In the first weeks and months, when everyone is around, trying to lift your spirits and keep you company, it is easy to be distracted, but when they are gone it becomes so much harder.

One of the things I missed the most was being picked up at the airport. It never mattered what time I landed, Steve would always be there.

I know it sounds a little crazy but, to this day, when I pick up my bags and start walking through the exit doors, a little part of me is still hoping to see him the other side . . . waiting with a great big hug.

For me, it was so desperately hard to move on. I, like many others, felt that moving on meant moving away, but I've realized now they are not the same. Moving on doesn't mean forgetting someone, it means allowing yourself to live again.

As someone who is a natural 'fixer' with very little patience, I've always had the answers, no matter how complex the problem. I've always been able to deal with things quickly: move on, start again, fix things, start things, end things.

Whatever needed to be done, I've been able to do it.

Losing Steve brought me to my knees, in so many ways, for

so many years. It made me realize, for the first time in my life, that I, too, am human. I, too, am mortal. I'm not invincible.

Losing someone so unexpectedly who has played such a deep, pivotal role in your life leaves an indelible mark.

However, the pain, over time and with the support of people who truly love you, does start to fade. Grief and loss have been my biggest life lesson. There are no shortcuts. I can't fix everything and I can't dictate the pace at which I heal. Believe me, I have tried.

My 'failure' at overcoming my grief undoubtedly led to successes elsewhere. It gave me the courage to leave behind the work everyone, including myself, thought I 'should' be doing and instead start doing the work I'd always wanted to do. The work I love.

I realized that life really is no dress rehearsal and that I can't live my life according to what other people want me to do, nor out of feelings of guilt or my sense of responsibility. I have to live it with passion and a deep-in-my-heart knowledge that this beautiful thing we call life is so very short and so very precious. I want my time to count.

I still struggle to believe that positives can come from such a loss, but I do see the light. It has made me a better person. More understanding, more tolerant, more open, more vulnerable, more giving. Not perfect, by any means, but more conscious that I'm not and that, indeed, none of us is.

At the same time, I suffer fools less gladly; I won't waste my time with people who are only out for themselves, I am not impressed by ego, status or wealth. I am, however, in awe of a person's heart and soul, for those are our true measure.

Above all, it has made me realize that the only thing that truly matters in our lives is the people we have in them. Love and friendship are our greatest gifts. Thank you to everyone who gives me theirs. As you read this, I ask one thing of you: take a moment to think . . .

Who could do with a hug today? Who could you call right now to tell them you love them? Who do you need to say sorry to? Who could you text just to tell them you're thinking about them? Who do you want to just say, 'Thanks for being you,' to? What little or big thing could you do for someone today that would mean the world to them?

Don't put it off until some 'tomorrow' . . . It may not arrive.

REDUNDANCY

I may not have experienced redundancy myself but, having worked with many people who have been through this, I really do think it can be a massive opportunity. It's a chance to take stock and really think about what you want to do and where your career is going.

I realize that, for most, it is also a shock, and the most natural reaction to shock is to panic. To think, *What am I going to do? How am I going to earn money?* Then the worst-case-scenario monkey brain kicks in and, before you know it, doom and gloom have settled. But it doesn't have to be like this. At all.

You will be given notice of a redundancy so, before it comes into effect, you will have time to start to think about your next steps. Most, if not all, redundancies come with a financial settlement package. Obviously, some are more generous than others but, regardless of the amount, see this as a chance to finally pursue what you've always wanted to do. You might not have all the money you need to make the absolutely perfect start to a new business or career transition. Sure, you might have to watch what you spend but, equally, this could give you a whole new lease of life.

See it as a little (or big) nudge to get you on the path that you've always wanted to be on but never quite got round to.

BANKRUPTCY

This is a hard pill to swallow for most, but you would be amazed how many very successful (and rich) business people have been bankrupt:

Here are a few random examples to get you started . . .

Donald Trump. OK, the less said here, the better.

Walt Disney. In his early career Walt struggled to pay his bills. The first company that he set up ended up in bankruptcy in 1923. Five years later he launched the character Mickey Mouse and, as they say, the rest is history!

Abraham Lincoln. When he was younger and before his political career he bought a shop in Illinois. It never really made money and, when his business partner died, he was left with all the debts. He lost all his assets and went bankrupt, continuing to pay off his debts for many years to come. In 1861 he became President of the United States – arguably, one of the best it has ever had.

Burt Reynolds was one of the biggest Hollywood stars in the 1970s and spent money like it was going out of fashion. By 1998 he had run out of money and finally declared bankruptcy.

Lady Gaga. During her 2009 Monsters Ball tour, she was technically bankrupt. She had thrown ALL her money into making it the ground-breaking stage that was to mark her out as one of the most popular artists of all time. Her argument was that by throwing all her money into her art, she would get the attention of the people who ran the tours and the industry. It worked. She received a $40 million cheque from Arthur Fogel and Live Nation after the tour. But if it hadn't worked . . .

Well, I'm sure she would have used this as a driver to get back up and go again.

The shock of a personal bankruptcy will no doubt set you back, at least to start with. It will certainly make it harder, although not impossible, to get loans or a mortgage. It will also undoubtedly make you think about money more. How you make it and how you keep it. I always believe that, if we learn our lesson from it, we can come back stronger.

That is definitely true for anyone who has experienced bankruptcy through their business. You will never make the same mistakes twice. One failed business does not make two or three failed businesses. In fact, it is far more likely to make your next business a greater success. You will be more prudent in saving your money, paying your taxes and keeping your overheads down and be more focused on generating sales, multiple streams of revenue and understanding the difference between profit and turnover.

CHAPTER TWO

MONEY SH*T

MONEY IS ONE OF THE MOST LOADED TOPICS WE CAN talk about. Money is a strange old thing, bits of paper and coins that in themselves have no real value and yet rule the world.

This chapter isn't about making money (although we'll touch on that), it's about our relationship with money. I would argue that it is our relationship to and the beliefs we have around money that determine how we create our money shit and how we fix it.

If we fundamentally believe that money is a bad thing, then it is unlikely that we are ever going to really make a lot of it or keep it. Most of our beliefs around money stem from our childhood – whether we were rich or poor, how our parents felt about money, whether they made it or lost it or just never had it.

We need to start challenging our thoughts around money if we're going to sort our shit out. Do we think rich people are bad or philanthropic? Do we believe that in order to make money we have to sacrifice our families, or that by making more money we are able to spend more time with our families? Like everything, we can find examples to prove both true.

As someone who grew up in a single-parent family on a

council estate with a teacher as a mother, I vowed I would never become a teacher. They are underpaid and under-appreciated. Oh, the irony: I am now a teacher. Just one who has figured out how to make money from doing it.

Many of us have at least some of these ingrained beliefs:

You have to be selfish to make money.

If you get rich, everyone wants something from you.

Only the rich get rich.

Money corrupts people.

If you want to get wealthy, you have to be prepared to sacrifice your family and friends.

Money is the root of all evil.

I'm not smart enough to make money.

I don't want to walk over people to get rich.

I'm sure you have your own to add to this list.

I absolutely love this quote from Jen Sincero in her brilliant book *You are a Badass at Making Money*:

> *'A healthy desire for wealth is not greed,*
> *it is a desire for life.'*

Money is both a commodity and a currency. It allows us greater choices: we get to choose what we do with that money. We could spend it all or give it all away. Or we could do a bit of both.

For me, the entire purpose of making money, aside from creating financial stability for my family, is to create as many wonderful memories as I can with the people I love. So that means I use my money to do so, but also to take the time off work.

In my world, there is no point in anything we are doing to make money if we aren't able to spend time with the people that we love and care about. I've really learned more and more over the years that hanging out with like-minded people who raise your spirit, lift your energy, help you grow, challenge you and help you make a bigger impact on the world, makes all the difference. That's what it's all about.

Because I am very clear about why I want to make money, it becomes easier to do so.

I grew up believing that rich people were selfish and greedy and that it was impossible for someone like me to become wealthy. Yet, as I went through life, I realized that the truth is that people are people and money is simply a magnifying glass. Generous people get to be more generous and selfish people become more selfish.

YOUR RELATIONSHIP WITH MONEY

'MONEY IS ONLY A TOOL. IT WILL TAKE YOU WHEREVER YOU WISH, BUT IT WILL NOT REPLACE YOU AS THE DRIVER.'

- AYN RAND

One thing I want to get really clear from the outset is that sorting your money shit out isn't just about making more money, although that helps. It's about sorting out what you think about money and your relationship with it. You may think that the answer is simply to make more money but, trust me, there are a lot of people who make more money than you who still have money shit to deal with; they just have bigger money problems to solve! And there is certainly no point in making more money, only to have no time to spend it.

GUILT

So many of us are frightened to truly invest in ourselves, particularly women.

We'll spend money on going out, on a new car, on alcohol, on all kinds of things – almost everything except ourselves. Our own personal or business development.

We're always thinking, *Oh God, can I afford it?*, yet we find the money for the new shoes, bags, clothes, the weekend drinks or the takeaway meals. It's always about priorities.

My good friend Sylvie, who now runs a multimillion-dollar business (from home), very nearly didn't start her own business through her money shit. She was earning great money working for a famous Hollywood actor and, as much as she loved it, her life wasn't her own, so she finally made the jump:

Before I made a dollar in my business I spent $2,000 on mentorship – not to mention all the other start-up costs. I remember that decision, $2,000 – it wasn't like me to just take my card out. It was a big decision. I had the cash in savings, but I'd worked my butt off for it. I was saving every penny by making homemade lattes, as you do when you're in a scarcity mindset and don't know how else you're gonna make or save money. I remember thinking, *But this isn't really for me, this is my kids' money. This is my family's money. Is this really gonna work? Am I good enough? How quickly will I see a return on my investment?*

I was the poster child for the martyr mum.

Thinking that all the money had to be for my kids actually did them a disservice. It wasn't teaching them the right lessons about money.

So, first of all, I had to make that decision: *Am I really going to do this? Is this going to be serious?* I could have bought a book for $25, but it would be a whole different experience. The fact that I made the investment was half of it. The simple act of pulling out the card and saying, 'OK, I'm doing it.' Well, how you gonna find the time? You work full time, have two toddlers and a teenager?! I don't know, I guess it's coming out of Netflix, going to have to get up at 5 a.m. I mean, you have to find the time; it's not gonna find you.

Until you've switched your mindset to believing that you're worth investing in, nothing changes.

You've got to start with the decision that you're worth it.

Luckily, you can make that decision right now. It's not like Santa . . . You don't have to wait until Christmas.

You just have to make a decision. You have to decide to change. You have to decide to grow. You have to decide that you want a better life. You have to decide that you want to start a business. You have to decide you want a better relationship. Then you have to take action on it.

Some people grow up thinking that money makes you selfish. I think it's the opposite. What is the point in anything that we're doing to make money if we aren't able to spend it on and with the people we love and care about?

It doesn't grow on trees,
but it does grow in some very strange places.

There's an old saying that you have to work hard enough to get rich enough not to have to work hard.

Now, I agree with this in principle . . . just like the harder you work, the luckier you get, but I also think things have changed with time. Money still doesn't grow on trees, but it has never been easier to make money in all kinds of ways doing all kinds of things . . . without ever leaving your living room. (Not that I would advise never leaving your living room.)

Before I get into the cornucopia of delights that is making money in the modern-day world, let's deal with a little reality.

Virtually everyone I know who is considered wealthy or rich has worked hard for it. Truth is, I don't know anyone who has a trust fund. The people I know, like me, typically started early – and I mean way before most people think about getting jobs. I was thirteen when I started work. Desperate to ride horses and with no money to do so, I cleaned out the stables. Small issue was I was hyper-allergic to horses and still am, so at the end of every day my face and neck would be covered in welts and I would be hardly able to breathe. I often wondered why my mum wasn't reported to the NSPCC. Joke. I was never going to let a little thing like an allergy or asthma stand in the way of something I really, really wanted.

I have worked since I was a teenager, every weekend and every school holiday. When everyone else was thinking about taking a gap year or partying, I was holding down two jobs. I started working full time while finishing my second year at university. The day I left uni, I started my first company. I worked long hours. I woke up early, went to bed late. Never watched TV, but I did party . . . and drink coffee. I made mistakes and had some major wins. I never gave up and I never gave up learning.

So before you start thinking about all the ways you can make extra money (trust me, there are literally millions of them), you need to decide whether you are really committed enough or whether this is just something else to talk about . . .

Even today, I wake up at 5.30 every day, including Sundays. I work harder than most people I know, but I LOVE what I do. Plus, I like to take a lot of time off!

So here are some examples of people who are currently making millions from their living rooms. I share these with you not because I expect you to want to do any of them; in fact, you might love working for someone else and really want to focus on your career progression (note: the same rules above apply). I share these stories because I want you to truly realize how today's world works and that you can make money out of anything. I want to start to dispel the myths that it's difficult to make money.

Charli's Crafty Kitchen: Two Australian sisters set this up in 2012 and by 2015 it was making $127,000 a month in ad revenue and sponsorship. By giving kids baking tutorials!

I Do Now I Don't: I Do Now I Don't was founded by Joshua Opperman and his sister Mara in 2007 as a peer-to-peer platform for selling expensive engagement and wedding rings that are no longer wanted. The idea came after Joshua's fiancée of three months left him, taking all of her belongings, apart from the ring; when he tried returning the ring to the retailer, he received a buy-back estimate that was about a third of the purchase price. In 2015, the company merged with Delgatto. Today, they sell about 1.7 million used engagement and wedding rings a year with a combined retail value of $4.2 billion.

Find focus groups: If you're the type of person who likes to share your opinions, you could earn around $150 per hour taking part in an online focus group, and quite possibly on some of your favourite topics. That means just sitting online responding to surveys, questionnaires or studies. With a bit of research and planning, you could easily earn a standard monthly salary without leaving your living room. You can find focus groups here: https://www.theworkathomewoman.com/money-focus-groups/

Vitality Air: In early 2015 Moses Lam and Troy Paquette filled a Ziploc bag with fresh air and posted it to eBay. The bag sold for 99 Canadian cents. So they filled another bag and posted that. After the media got hold of the story, a bidding war began – it sold for C$168. In June 2015 Vitality Air sold its first canister. A few months later the company received an order for

5,000 cans, which were shipped exclusively to cities in China. As of November 2017, they have sold over 200,000 bottles at around C$32 a pop! I know – I don't believe it either!

So the moral of the story is, whether you want a promotion at work, to start your own company or just to make some extra on the side, none of it will happen if you don't do any . . . work.

CHAPTER THREE
RELATIONSHIP SH*T

BEING MINDFUL OF
THE WRONG PEOPLE

I know we're supposed to believe that everyone is created equal but, personally, I find that a struggle to agree with. I get the theory, but in practice it just doesn't work out that way.

Part of being an adult is having the choice about which people we are going to spend time with. Who are we going to prioritize? Whose feelings, opinions and thoughts are we going to take into consideration, especially when there are opposing ones?

One of the choices you'll regret for ever is being mindful of the wrong people and prioritizing them. Maybe even putting these people above yourself and your own happiness. So you need to think carefully about who you are mindful of.

Are you mindful of the people who support you? The ones who have your back? Who are truly there for you?

Or are you mindful of the people who create drama and chaos in your life in the hope that, by being so, it will somehow limit the damage? Are you being mindful of people because you fear that, if you don't give in to them and give them what they want, they're just going to create more havoc and disruption?

Tip: This never, ever works.

Let's face it: when we do this, we do it because we're scared. We don't have the courage to stand up to such people and do what's right, so we give in.

I've been guilty of this in the past, but not for a very long time. I was guilty of being mindful of the people who would cause me headaches; in fact, I was more mindful of them than I was of the people who helped take my headaches away. How crazy is that?

It's like some kind of reverse psychology. I'd be mindful of the people who I thought were going to cause me problems because I didn't want any more stress or drama in my life. I thought, *Well, do you know what? Let me prioritize those people because, if I do that, then I'm not going to get any more headaches*. OMG. How wrong could I be?! It literally had the opposite effect: it just made these people think that they could walk all over me.

And in the process of being mindful of those people, I wasn't mindful of the people who really counted.

I took them for granted because they *didn't* give me any headaches.

Then, when I lost my partner, I realized that all the time I had wasted pussyfooting around people for fear of headaches and dramas had just made my life more stressful. And wasted so much time.

We need to stop caring about the wrong people, stop caring what's happening in the lives of people who really don't care about what's happening in our lives, and instead start caring more about the people who care about us. We need to start caring more about what we think about ourselves instead of what other people think of us. How about we stop being mindful of the wrong people and start being mindful of ourselves? How about we start treating ourselves with the love and respect we want other people to treat us with? That would be a great place to start.

Truth is, some people just don't get life. These people are in a cycle. Like *Groundhog Day*. They talk about stuff, but they don't do it. They just keep doing all the same stuff that they keep telling everyone they don't want to do any more. They keep eating unhealthily, keep drinking, keep smoking, not exercising. They stay stuck in a job they don't enjoy and in a relationship they don't want to be in.

And the next week is the same, and the week after is the same. And six months later it's the same. These people stay exactly where they are for ever because they choose what's easy over what's really important. Don't be that person. And if you've been guilty of being that person before, it's time to change.

Even if everything I've just said sounded like you, even if you are overweight, in a shitty relationship and smoking twenty a day, even if you hate your job and have for the last five years, you have a choice right now to stop. We can all make that choice. We can all make better choices. If you only have one or two things to change, then celebrate, because it is easy once you commit to it.

Here's to making choices we don't regret. Here's to making choices we embrace, to celebrating our choices and being damn freaking proud of them. That's my goal in life: to make choices I'm proud of. Will I always get it right? I doubt it. I'm a work in progress, just like you. But I'm conscious of the choices and decisions I make so, when I make bad decisions, I'm quick to do something about it.

Here's to courage. To vulnerability. To appreciating ourselves. And here's to making the kind of choices that, when we get to the end of our lives, instead of looking back with regret, we just look back with pride.

HOW TO AVOID NEGATIVE PEOPLE

Let me explain something about negative people – and whether they are your friends, your family or your partner, the same rule applies. We have positive energy, and we have negative energy. We have energy vampires who literally suck the life out of us, and we have people who just light our souls on fire.

It's time to take stock and get rid of the negativity, get rid of the vampires, get rid of anybody in your life who isn't there to support you. Now, please recognize what I'm saying. This does not mean that the people you want to be with should agree with everything you say or do. Far from it. The people who light up my soul don't think that every idea I have is brilliant or that I walk on water. In fact, when they think I'm doing something wrong, they are very quick to tell me, and so they should. These are the people who really love you. These are the people who fan your flames.

What you don't want is people who are always looking for the negative. Who find five problems for every solution. Who tell you that every idea you have 'won't work', or that it's 'too difficult', or even laugh when you suggest it.

Just because something won't work for them does not mean it won't work for you.

You see, here's what happens when you start to make changes and take a leap into the future. You make other people feel uncomfortable. Your new-found decisiveness means that your life is going to start to change, and that makes people start to think about their own lives.

When I decided to get really fit, I was amazed how many well-meaning people would say things to me like, 'Oh, Sháá, I think you've lost too much weight,' or 'Make sure you don't get obsessive with your exercise.' I mean, seriously? Firstly, exercising four times a week is not obsessive, it's good for you.

Secondly, it's hardly like I'm getting excessive about downing a bottle of Prosecco every night!

I'm thinking to myself, *I'm in the best freaking shape of my life. Please don't tell me what I need to be doing or not.* But of course, it wasn't about me, it was about them. Me losing weight made them think about the fact that they might need to lose weight, too.

It's a really bizarre thought process, but some people prefer to keep others down so they feel better about themselves. Whether it's your weight or your career progression, the moment you start to 'overtake' them, they become a Debbie Downer, giving you all the reasons why you are better off not making these changes. You'll see it in relationships, too: you rarely find someone who is happy in their own relationship advising you against being in one. But if someone isn't happy in their own personal life, they'll be the first to give you all the negatives about moving in with your partner, getting married or making any kind of commitment.

If someone isn't championing you in every area of your life, they don't deserve a place in your life.

BE CAREFUL WHO YOU SPEND TIME WITH

'SET YOUR LIFE ON FIRE.
SEEK THOSE WHO FAN YOUR FLAMES.'

- RUMI

I am utterly convinced that following this rule my whole life and doing my best to fan others' flames is what has bought me the greatest joy, happiness and success.

I recently watched a Will Smith video as I was scrolling through Facebook (yes, I'm guilty of it, too, but I do have 'most' of my shit sorted) and I found it very poignant. Here's a little snippet of what he had to say:

> The prerequisite for spending time with any person is that they nourish and inspire you, they feed your flame. If they don't, spend more time with those that do. Stop right now and go and look at your last five text messages: are they feeding your flames or dousing your fire? Look around you and the people you spend your time with. Whether it's your friends, your family or at work. Are they people throwing logs on your fire or pissing on it? The people that you spend time with will make or break your dreams. Everybody doesn't deserve to be around you. You have to defend your light with your life.

And therein lies the secret to life. If people aren't throwing logs on your fire, remove them from your life. Spend more time with fewer people who truly light you up. Even better, spend time with the people who, when your light has gone out, are the first to come round with the logs, the kindling and the matches. The people who not only set your life on fire but will never let it die out.

NEVER LET ANYONE CHANGE YOU

I've seen a lot of conversations online recently about people feeling let down by other people's behaviour. I've seen it happen in groups, in friendships and in relationships.

The human reaction is to take a step back, to question why. Why you? Are you a walkover? Is your judgement faulty?

Maybe you trust people too much?

We've grown up being taught that trust is something that is earned. Yet I've always had the opposite view: I will trust people until they prove that I can't.

Maybe it's foolish. I know for sure that there are occasions where, in hindsight, I wish I hadn't.

When I look at those individual situations, I could say to myself, *I should have waited for that person to 'earn' my trust before I gave it and everything else so freely.*

Yet still I refuse to change.

I always see the best in people because I believe, when you do that, 99 per cent of them will rise to the potential that you see. One per cent won't.

Don't change for the 1 per cent.

And who knows, maybe the 1 per cent will look back at your kindness, trust and support and realize *that* was their moment. To learn, to grow, to win. And they chose not to.

Changing in this sense means that you allow the very people who have ridden roughshod over your kind, giving and supportive nature to change you.

Don't do that.

Changing means that you start judging everyone by the lowest common denominator, and not the highest.

You start expecting the worst from people instead of the best.

You pull back. You give less.

But that also means you become less.

Become more, not less.

ADULTING, AKA PARENTING

We all want to do our best by our kids. All of us.

But sometimes, the very decisions we think we are making in their best interests could be the very worst. Our decisions are setting them up to follow in our footsteps. To see our choices and decision-making as routes that they, too, should follow.

It's no surprise that children whose parents smoke are much more likely to smoke themselves. Children who grow up with parents who have addictions are eight times as likely to become addicts themselves. Children who grow up with parents who are abusive tend to either become abusive or end up in abusive relationships.

I know these examples probably seem extreme for most people, but what about the things we put up with in our day-to-day lives? What examples are we setting there?

That it's OK not to follow your dreams?

That it's OK to stay in a job you don't enjoy because that's better than rocking the boat at home?

That it's OK to stay poor because others believe that, if you want to have money or pursue your dreams, you have to do it at the expense of your family? That, of course, is total NONSENSE.

When our kids see us settling in any area of our lives, that sets the bar for what they think they are worth, too. So if you think you're unworthy, your kids are likely to grow up thinking the same thing about themselves.

They see you putting your dreams on hold for other people; they'll never pursue theirs.

They see you wasting your time and your life; they'll do the same.

They see you up all night gaming or surfing the Web with no real direction in life; they'll do the same.

They see you thinking that, because I come from this background, with that history, this is all that is possible for me; they'll think the same.

They see your world as small; so will theirs be.

They see you in a job rather than truly pursuing your dreams – guess what? They will settle, too. They will give up their dreams. They will give in because they've seen you do the same thing.

YOU are the one who sets the example for what your kids will believe is possible for them.

Not through words. Through actions.

If you knew for sure that the way you showed up in life, the dreams you pursued or didn't pursue, the chances you took or didn't take and the way you lived your life were going to be replicated by your kids . . . would you do the same thing? Would you carry on settling? Would you carry on putting off until tomorrow what you want to do today?

I may not be good at everything but, on this, I can look myself in the mirror and there is not much I would change.

My son, Jett, will know for sure that, even if his mother got it wrong and made many mistakes along the way, her life was lived and loved full out.

His mum was a doer, not a talker. A fighter, not a runner. She was someone who never believed in living her life by other people's limitations.

Her past didn't define her, her future did.

That is the greatest gift we can give our kids.

Courage.

CHAPTER FOUR

HEALTH SH*T

ONE OF THE MOST COMMON AREAS THAT PEOPLE NEED TO fix is their health. I'm not talking critical illness here but, if you're not careful, that's what it could lead to.

I'm talking about the long-term neglect of our bodies (and our minds); the choice to put our health low on our priority list because the assumption is that we can get to it tomorrow.

Almost all of us take our health for granted because we have it . . . But when something goes wrong it becomes our number-one priority and we would give anything to turn back the clock and change it.

Things like smoking, drinking and fast food are habitual and, of course, it's hard to break a habit, but the long-term risks far outweigh the commitment and dedication needed to quit. If you sit there and think you can get away with it and that the bad stuff only happens to other people, you're wrong. On the day you find that out, you will wish with all your heart that you had done something about it earlier . . . like, right now. So, while I'm here, in your corner, do something about it this minute. Get that number for AA or the NHS quit-smoking line and make that call . . . I'll wait while you do . . . Don't smoke or drink, but just know you're not in your best shape? Sign up to a gym, book a full body MOT. Take a step. A big step in the right direction.

It is not only possible, it is entirely doable to be healthy in body, mind and spirit, no matter where you are at right now. Sounds like the holy grail, right? But, with determination, by getting your priorities right and with a good dose of consistency, you can and will do it.

MIND

If you really want to sort out your health shit, it all starts with the mind, and the most important place to start there is with acceptance. Accept that we are all going to have shit days, days when we feel unhappy and days when life just keeps on testing us. If we accept that, then it is so much easier to take those moments, days or even weeks in our stride because we know that they are part of everyone's life, including our own.

Mindfulness and meditation seem to be today's go-to cure-alls but, I'll be honest, they don't necessarily work for me. Or at least not in the traditional way. I have tried to meditate on many occasions, bought every app in the App Store and still couldn't calm my monkey brain. I'm a big believer in finding what's right for you and I fully believe in the principles of both mindfulness and meditation, so I find a way that works for me. Instead of traditional meditation, I practise active meditation. I run naked. Not without clothes, but without music! This helps both clear and calm my brain like nothing else can.

Personally, I have found that the best way for me to 'meditate' is by swimming in an outdoor pool – ideally, alone. I realize that this is both totally idyllic and impossible to turn into a daily practice, especially when you live in London!

However, what I know for sure is that my best ideas for both business and my books have come from swimming outdoors, by myself, in a beautiful location. This could also be my mind playing tricks on me to justify extra holidays!

The point is, you have to find what works for you and, if you can't swim in an infinity pool every day in the tropical heat, then you have to find the next best thing. For me, that's running. Anywhere, in any weather.

I just have to ditch the music because, as much as I love Drake, my thoughts are too wrapped up in his lyrics to zone out. Running without music creates the perfect environment for my brain to settle down. The rhythmic nature of it provides a background for my thoughts to tap into with absolutely no distraction. When I sit and meditate, I find it impossible to corral my busy thoughts, yet when I'm running they seem to just vanish. Find what works for you and don't judge yourself too harshly if your way is different to others'; there is no right or wrong and there are no better ways. There is just the way that works for you.

When it comes to being mindful, I'm a gratitude kinda gal. That means I make it a daily habit to show people that I care and that I'm grateful for their love and support. It could be a little thing like a random text or, even better, a personal card or buying tickets to a concert I know someone will love. Acknowledging what we have to be grateful for is a great way to help you fix your shit because it focuses on the positive. It also gives you more strength and momentum to tackle your problems head on.

For me personally, though, I find it makes the biggest difference to do something. People can't read your mind. They don't know that you are grateful if you don't show them or tell them. It's not about money and it doesn't have to be extravagant gestures. It's the thought that counts, so the key is to have more thoughts.

Tip: Two good friends of mine, Alex Ikonn and UJ Ramdas, created the Five-minute Journal, and it is a great way to spend the first five minutes of your day writing down what you are grateful for. This really helps bring some perspective back into your life.

If you're like me and you struggle with traditional meditation, don't give up on the concept, just change the practice. You could try naked running, or just get outside for a while. Spending too many hours in front of a computer screen isn't good for our mental or physical wellbeing.

Reconnecting with nature allows your body and your mind to recalibrate. It doesn't matter whether it's a walk in the park, along a beach or just somewhere away from the daily grind.

Our senses are literally bombarded all day long with messages, DMs, PMs, advertising, conversations, sounds . . . It's hard to find a peaceful moment, yet our peaceful moments are where our deepest and most profound changes come from.

These moments will give us far more clarity than anything else.

HOW TO GET YOUR MOJO BACK

There are times when even the most positive of us lose our mojo, if only momentarily . . . So here are some simple ways to get it back . . .

1. Cut out all the people and things that don't make your soul truly sing. Sounds simple, right, but it's not necessarily as easy as it sounds. If you're anything like me, you always try to see the best in people. Truth is, some people are just not worth having around your fire. Fortunately, the world is full of people who are. Find them and hold them tight.

2. Now reverse this . . . Remind yourself of all the people and things that make you happy. Spend more

time with them. Pick up the phone, plan something, schedule something. Don't just talk about it, do it. Nothing helps you get your mojo back more quickly than being around positive, like-minded people. People who actually DO something, not just talk about something. The people who build you up and champion you. I truly believe you are the sum of the five people you spend the most time with. Take a good look around . . .

3. Get outside. Go for a run, or a walk. Get some fresh air. Go somewhere with uninterrupted views. Go to a beach. Need to travel two hours to do it? It's more than worth the effort. If you live in a city, constantly being surrounded by buildings, especially in the grey of winter, can make you feel claustrophobic. Our hearts, minds and souls need space to breathe . . . and space to let our mojo back in.

4. Do something. Stop thinking about all the stuff that's bothering you and start doing something about it. Taking action, even imperfect action, puts you back in control. When we lose our mojo, we feel out of control; we can't quite find our footing. Action helps you get a grip.

Remember: it's YOUR mojo. Don't let someone take it away from you.

BODY

Today, I am fitter than I was when I was twenty-five. I'm leaner, stronger and faster.

This didn't happen by accident, it happened by fixing my shit.

A friend of mine had, it would be fair to say, a substantial amount of weight to lose: more than 120lb. She lives in America and I had been watching her progress on Facebook for a few months. Week by week, month by month, she was consistently dropping the pounds. I sat there feeling slightly uncomfortable, carrying an extra 20lb that I didn't need or want, but I could still fit into a UK size 12 so I decided it couldn't be that bad. Therein lies the problem: not fixing things until they really are that bad.

One day I opened FB and the first pic I saw was of Rachel, and I swear she only had 20lb to lose and she was going to be the same size as me! I was in both shock and awe. In awe of her accomplishment and in shock that I had spent the last four months just watching her FB feeds and doing nothing. That FB post got me to the threshold of changing my physical fitness quicker than anything else I've ever known. I'm sure the competitive part of me also had something to do with it.

Now here is a lesson in eliciting quick but lasting change, without ever giving your monkey brain a chance to second-guess you.

I picked up the phone and called her straight away. I was totally honest: I said I couldn't believe her determination and results. I asked her to tell me what she was doing. So she started to tell me she had been working with a trainer in Austin, Texas, who had a programme called Fat Stalker (he basically stalks all your food and exercise, leaving no place to hide . . . or lie!). So I got his name and, while she was telling me the rest, I had googled him, found his website and his programme. Before she had finished telling me about it, I had already put my PayPal details in and was a fully paid-up member! She then told me about her Polar M430 watch which tracked all her exercise each day – yep, you guessed it, I was on Amazon ordering as we spoke. Then she pinged me the food list – all the things you could have and couldn't have. I hung up the phone, went into the kitchen, got out a great big bin bag and went through every cupboard, my fridge and my freezer and threw away EVERYTHING that wasn't on the list of foods you could eat. The only food left was my son's cereals and snacks, as I never ate them anyway.

Within fifteen minutes, I had signed up to her coach, bought my watch and thrown away all the food that wasn't on the list. This is how you get results. By going all in.

You find someone who has achieved the results you want to achieve and you find out how they got them. Then you go and model EXACTLY what they did. Do not expect the same results with half the effort!

Next up, I called David (the trainer) and realized I had literally signed my life away! Every day I had to send him a picture of my scales and a screenshot of both my exercise for the day (as tracked by my watch, so you can't cheat, and my food intake, as tracked by MyFitnessPal. Now, you could try to hack this, but it just wouldn't work.

The watch doesn't just track your steps, it tracks your heartbeat, so it knows and shows how hard you worked or how far and how fast you ran. Sure, you could lie about what you ate, but the scales would dob you in!

I know some of you may be reading this and thinking to yourself that this seems incredibly strict. It is!!! In fact, I call it binary. You either do it, or you don't do it. Simple. Get results or make excuses. You can't do both.

I honestly think this approach works in every area of our lives, not just our fitness. Modelling, or mirroring, as some people call it, is the process of finding someone who has achieved what you want to achieve and simply copying what they did and how they did it.

It won't suit everyone, and it may not be for you, but there will be something out there that will work for you, so when you see it, grab it and follow it through.

Who would have thought that there would be a day when

someone from the other side of the world could impact our fitness and health on such a significant scale – without ever being in the same room as you? Now don't get me wrong, it wasn't a walk in the park (more like a daily four-mile run!) and it took a lot of discipline from me, too, but mostly, like everything else that works, it took consistency.

For so many years we have fallen into the trap of believing that we hit a certain age and then everything changes. The best is behind us. I call bullshit on that. I look just as good, if not better, than I did twenty years ago. It's time to redefine the rules and decide what you really want. You want to be fitter than you've ever been? You absolutely can do that. I am living testament. I am a single mum who was 20lb overweight on a tiny five-foot four-inch frame, I had asthma (past tense – that's gone now, too!), I'm a widow and I run multiple businesses. I didn't have a PT or home-delivered calorie-counted meals, but what I did have was the desire to make my body a priority. After all, it's the only one I've got.

DRINKING

Now I'm going to give you a little heads-up here . . . I am a non-drinker. As in, I have never drunk. Well, when I was fourteen, someone got me to try whisky, and I thought it tasted like paint stripper, so that was the beginning and end of it. Now why do I say this to you? Well, firstly, because I accept that, as someone who has never drunk alcohol, let alone experienced a hangover, it would be easy for people to make an assumption that I have no clue what having a drinking problem is like. Or why people do it.

On the contrary, I grew up with a father who was both a drug user and an alcoholic. I make the choices I make because of how I grew up.

We should be very clear that while 'social' drinking is widely accepted, the truth is, alcohol has very severe health consequences. The fact that this information is so widely available and accepted makes it all the worse.

In 2015 Professor Kevin Moore of the Royal Free Hospital, London, co-authored a massive study on the effects of a four-week break from alcohol. The participants were average drinkers and the results were, literally, unbelievable.

By the end of the four weeks the participants had each lost, on average, 40 per cent of their liver fat and 6–7lb in weight. They had also reduced their cholesterol and lowered their glucose levels, as well as experiencing many other health improvements.

Moore was so impressed with the findings he suggested that, if there were a pill that produced similar results, everyone would want it.

But this wasn't about a magic pill or a strategy that had to do with the actual drinking of alcohol, it was about the mindset behind the reason the participants claimed led them to drink, their belief system about what drinking enabled them to be or do.

The participants believed alcohol enabled them to be the best version of themselves. They believed they became more:

Successful

Popular

Bold

In control

In order to stop the habit, they had to change the habits and patterns they had built up around their drinking. Years of social conditioning and self-doubt had to be unpacked so that they could become strong and independent regardless of outside substances.

The study revealed that addictions are caused by a lack of

self-love and lack of self-moderation; it's never about just removing the stimulant or depressant, but rather about rebuilding the person so they don't need the 'addiction' to be their best self.

> *'Bad habits don't need telling off, they need replacing.'*
> *– One Year, No Beer*

It is crucial to learn how to create the image of your ideal self and life and use it to change your trajectory towards success in all areas of your life. Realizing that you can do this on your own terms not only takes away the vices that people lean on but also enables you to make changes far more easily because you are more likely to trust in the process of change.

As always, mindset comes first.

SMOKING

Fortunately, the percentage of people smoking continues to drop year on year. In some ways, that is no surprise, as the evidence of the fatal consequences are now so well documented it would be impossible for anyone to deny them. If, however, you are among the 1 per cent or so of the population who still smoke, then I think it's time to fix that shit.

Like all bad habits, the best way to get rid of it is to replace it with a better one. That is why vapes and E-cigarettes have become so popular. That said, there is now evidence that they carry their own health warnings. Obviously, the best thing to do is simply give up, but I realize it's not as easy as that.

Truth is, different things work for different people. Some swear by hypnosis, others by gradually weaning themselves off through the use of patches.

The biggest shift in smoking has come about since 2007, when most of Europe, including the UK, created a ban on smoking in all public places (in the UK, this now includes your car). As smoking became less and less socially acceptable (unlike drinking), the numbers of people smoking dropped dramatically.

Sadly, though, your social background still plays the largest part in your decision to either smoke, not smoke or give up. People living in the most deprived areas of England are four times more likely to smoke than those in the least deprived areas.

According to new analysis by the Office for National Statistics (ONS) and Public Health England, the next most important factors were whether people grew up with parents who smoked. Unsurprisingly, those who grew up with smokers as parents were nearly six times more likely to become smokers themselves. (The same is true for alcohol abuse.)

Perhaps the most frightening of all the statistics is that a person is also more likely to smoke if they reported having a health problem, like difficulty with breathing, shortness of breath or even chronic obstructive pulmonary disease (COPD). The NHS estimates that smoking is responsible for nine out of ten cases of COPD and 85 per cent of cases of lung cancer. Deaths from respiratory diseases, including COPD, are more than twice as common in smokers.

You can't argue with these statistics.

EATING

If you're like the vast majority of the population, your eating habits could probably be improved. Now, before you think I am holier than thou, I still have to keep my own eating habits in check; otherwise, trust me, I'd be eating baked Alaska every night.

With so many things pulling on our time, we have become increasingly reliant on quick and easy food, otherwise known as takeaways or ready-meals.

The latest NHS figures show that more than half of the British population is overweight or obese. That's 65 per cent of men and 58 per cent of women. On average, British adults consume 200–300 calories a day MORE than they need. It takes roughly 3,500 calories to add 1lb of weight, so you can see how easy it is to stack up the pounds.

And it's not just the calories. The average ready-meal has over 600 calories in one dish and TWICE the sugar content of a regular can of Coke!

Like exercise, eating right is about finding out what works for you. It doesn't matter whether you're a meat eater or a vegan, you can find the path that's right for you, just take what you put into your body seriously. If you want to lose weight, 90 per cent of it will be down to what you eat, not how you exercise.

It's never too late to change your eating habits. Never. Today is always a good day to start.

CHAPTER FIVE

WORK SHI*T

HOW TO TOTALLY REINVENT YOURSELF

I doubt there is anyone reading this right now who hasn't at some point thought about doing something different.

Maybe even being someone different.

Stuck in an office as a bookkeeper but really want to be a personal trainer? Or maybe you're a teacher and you really want to be a beekeeper? Always dreamed of running your own business, but it's still just a dream? Or just want to run away with the circus . . . literally and figuratively? Want more money, a promotion or simply some recognition?

Well, the good news is that, today, it is entirely possible to reinvent yourself, to change your career and your life.

Here are five tips to get you started:

1. Recognize that, just because you were good at maths at school, it does not mean you need to be an accountant, a financial director or anything else related to numbers for the rest of your life. Unless you want to, of course. Maybe you love writing, or make the best vegan brownies, or have helped

countless friends set up their own businesses. If so, it might be time to step out of the box you've been stuck in and start making money doing something you really love.

2. Don't worry about how old you are or how many years you've invested in your current career. Truth is, you can carry all that knowledge into the career that you really want to pursue. Those skills will not be wasted, they will be repurposed. And remember, Ray Kroc was in his fifties when he set up McDonald's. Never let age be a barrier to making the rest of your life the best of your life.

3. Create a really clear plan for your transformation. Consider everything. Do you need to learn new skills? How are you going to fund it? Can you scale back what you're currently doing to three days a week so you can have a couple of days a week dedicated to the new project? The more you prepare, the easier it will be.

4. Begin before you are ready. Don't wait for the perfect moment. Start now. Make a plan. Start working on it at the weekends, evenings or in whatever spare time you can grab.

5. Utilize social media to create a platform for your new venture. You can start this while you're still doing your old 'thing'. In fact, documenting your journey from worn-out accountant to passionate PT is a great way to build your tribe. People will be attracted to you not just because of what you do but why you're doing it. Sharing your journey will help you stand out from the crowd, give you a real head start and attract exactly the clients you want: people like you.

So what are you waiting for? There has never been a better time to reinvent yourself.

DOING YOUR OWN THING

Not everyone should start a business, but I believe everyone would benefit from becoming an entrepreneur, or at least having the mindset of an entrepreneur.

The standard definition of the word (see below) would lead people to believe that they have to be a big risk-taker, the type who's prepared to bet the farm on 'black' in order to get things started. However, in my twenty-odd years of being an entrepreneur, this is rarely the case. It's much more about a mindset.

Entrepreneur, noun: a person who sets up a business or businesses, taking on financial risks in the hope of profit.

I think the bestselling author Guy Kawasaki puts it much better:

'"Entrepreneur" is not a job title. It's the state of mind of people who want to alter the future.'

Now, most of us want to alter our future for the better, and being entrepreneurial in both our thinking and our money-making ventures increases our chances of doing so. Some of us want to set up our own business while others would like to earn some extra income on the side or get a promotion. All require an entrepreneurial mindset. One of my friends has a stable career in local government, but in the last year she has become focused on getting healthier and, as part of that, she started running retreats to help other stressed-out executives switch off for a few days. This in no way impacts on her day job, nor does it make her enough money to quit, but it has given her a nice holiday fund.

Maybe you've got a hobby that you love: cooking, baking cakes, art, throwing parties, helping people write up business plans . . . These are all great ways to hone your entrepreneurial talent. You don't have to be all or nothing. You don't have to quit your job or work sixty hours a week to be an entrepreneur; you just have to start thinking differently. Look for opportunities where you can start to alter your future for the better . . .

You can always start part time; this can mean on the side of a main job, while you're on maternity leave or just a day or two a week. Test the water before diving in. Work from home. Keep your costs low and stash the extra cash. You could even rent out your spare room on Airbnb or longer term, and get some great tax benefits.

Have a clear-out . . . Yes, I know this isn't exactly setting up a business on the side, but it is entrepreneurial because you are literally making money out of old rope . . . or old clothes, old toys, old bags. Our homes are bursting at the seams with all the 'stuff' we possess and no longer use, and yet most of us could also use some spare cash.

It's like a double win . . . You get more space and more cash. Then you can invest the cash in a new venture . . . or a new wardrobe.

So, if you've decided you're ready to do your own thing, here's my simple seven-step guide to making it happen . . .

1.

FIND YOUR PURPOSE

Yep, I know you've heard all this before, but hear me out. If you don't know why you're doing this, or what you're aiming for, it will be far too easy to be put off course. Your purpose doesn't have to be anything grandiose; it might simply be to create an income around your kids or to put into practice an idea you've had for years.

It might mean that you want to empower the world to eat more healthily, work less, be financially free . . . or maybe you're just the best handbag designer on the planet!

So, what's your purpose? And what's the purpose of this business? They may be the same thing but, equally, they might not be. The key is to make sure your business reflects your true skills, passion and, yes, purpose.

2.

YOUR BUSINESS MAP

After brainstorming, you'll probably have plenty of ideas floating around. Now is the time to put them together, in a plan. Yes, a business plan, but I prefer to think of it as a map. You don't need a 200-page business plan that you lock in a drawer, you need a map to get you from here to there. It should give you an overview of all aspects of your business – where you will make money and when, what additional skills you need to bring on board and key milestones along the way.

This bit might sound boring, but it's actually really important. If you want to get to your Caribbean island, you need a map.

3.
ASK FOR HELP

Even the most talented people will struggle to do everything. The best way to create an extraordinary business you love running is to focus on the bits you love and find other people to fill in the gaps. One of the best things you can do at this stage is to recognize your strengths and outsource, or look for help, in other areas.

For example, if your creative and leadership skills are excellent but your admin skills leave a little to be desired, you might consider hiring a virtual assistant to give you a helping hand. There are so many online resources to help you find the right freelancers, no matter what the job is.

4.

FIND YOUR CLIENTS

What does your ideal client look like?
What do they do? Where do they hang out? Not
sure how to find them? Think about who you get
the best results with right now and who you love
working with the most.
Once you know who your ideal client is, it will be
much easier to find them – then you can start
tailoring your marketing to exactly those people.
No point being a jack of all trades and master of
none. Working with your ideal clients will make
you a much happier person and give you a more
profitable business.

5.

KNOW YOUR WORTH

You've got your product or service, you know what
your costs should be, and you know who your
target market is. Now – how much should you
charge? Research how much your competitors are
charging, what people are willing to pay for a
similar service.
If you're still not sure what to charge and you're
offering a service, consider the following: work
out how much you would honestly want (and
realistically expect) to earn in a year, then break it

down to a monthly and hourly rate. As long as this covers your costs and allows you a profit margin, you're close to the right figure – at least, to get you started.

6.
KEEP ON LEARNING

As you embark on a new journey, it's important to keep learning to improve your skills and gain new ones. Sign up for a course. Go to a workshop. Read a book. Never stop learning.

7.
DEALING WITH YOUR NEGATIVE INNER VOICE

OK, so let's get real. There are going to be times when that little voice inside your head says, *Are you sure you're doing the right thing?*, *Isn't this risky?* or *This feels like too much hard work* . . . You know that voice? We all do.

You have to learn how to switch it off. The more you think about it, the louder it will be, so the trick is to acknowledge the voice – and then, very firmly, tell it to shut up.

To make this easier, surround yourself with positive people who are already doing what you want to

do, or who are at least on a similar path; they will
be the voice of reason when you need one. If you
don't have people like that in your life, then come
and join my free Facebook group, The Freedom
Collective (shaa.com/freedom), which is filled with
entrepreneurs, small businesses and people
wanting to make a difference in their lives.

HOW TO FAST-TRACK YOUR CAREER

Starting your own business isn't the answer for everyone, but I
am a big believer in encouraging everyone, no matter what
they do or where they work, to become more entrepreneurial.

So how do you fix your work shit if you have less control over
it? If you work for someone else instead?

Well, the same rules apply. Firstly, you've got to figure out
what your shit is that needs fixing, then map out a plan.

Have no plans to set up your own business but don't like your
current career path? Figure out what you want to do instead
and find people who are already doing it. Reach out to them,
ask them for advice and help. How did they get started? What
were the break-out points for them? Also, be practical: can you
earn enough money in this new career or will your earnings
take a dive for a couple of years? If that is the case, it doesn't
mean you shouldn't pursue it, but you do need to be realistic.
How are you going to handle that? Scale down, take in a lodger,
get a second job? Everything is possible, but you have to have
a plan to make it so.

Maybe you love the career you're in but you'd just like to be making a bit more money. Then get clear on how much more money that is and who in your profession is earning it. What are they doing differently to you? Is it just their seniority or is it that they work for a larger company?

Have they had to sell their soul to the devil? (OK, a little extreme, but if they are working seventy hours a week to earn an extra 20k a year, I'd suggest finding alternative ways to make the 20k.)

Do you have a plan for your own promotion? How often are you applying for new roles, whether in your existing company or outside of it? You don't always have to move company to get a promotion, but you tend to earn more money by doing so. What about training? If you're in a corporate company, they are often willing to give you the opportunity to train for new skills, as it benefits them, too . . . and they'll pay for it. It's a win–win situation, as you learn something and increase your earning potential, should you want more career opportunities.

If you absolutely love where you work, then start to track ways that you can help make or save your company more money. Instead of acting like an employee, act like an entrepreneur. Bring ideas to the table and make yourself indispensable, no matter what your role. Prove the value that you bring to the business, and not just anecdotally: track the results of what you do in the business to demonstrate the company's return on its investment in employing you.

Being proactive like this will make any company stand up and take notice. They will not want to lose an employee who is not just bringing real value into their business but one who is also proactively looking at ways in which they can contribute more.

Remember, financial remuneration is only part of your package, albeit an important one. Maybe you can negotiate longer holidays, extra days working from home, private medical cover. All of these things will help put you in a better position to fix the rest of your shit . . . and once you've got the work shit nailed, it gives you more time to focus on sorting out the rest!

WHY BUSINESS ISN'T ABOUT FACTS, FIGURES, GOALS AND TARGETS

When I started out, I drove a Honda. To be honest, it was a shitty car, but let's face it, I was twenty-one and it's all I could afford. I used to drive around in that car and, every time I got in, I'd tell myself, 'One day, I'm going to buy a Range Rover.'

I bought my first one at twenty-six, my second at thirty-four and my current beauty earlier this year. When I ordered this car, I went all out. I made it bespoke. All-black everything. Rims, wheels, interior. Upgraded stereo. All-glass roof.

I earned it. Not just financially, but through blood, sweat and tears. Late nights and early mornings. Never giving up.

Always fighting, never running.

Ever.

No, it's not all about money, but I tell you what, there is no shame in making money and there is no pride in being poor. There is certainly no legacy to be left for our children in them watching us play small. Or hiding from our potential.

Yeah, I know some people think business is about facts, figures, goals and targets, but it's not. The people who say this have never run a business. And, with all due respect, they are probably never going to achieve a fraction of their potential if that's what they believe.

To the contrary, business is about:

Integrity

Emotions

Dignity

Morals

Courage

Feelings

Reliability

Consistency

Resilience

Loyalty

Vision

Choices

Strength

Determination

Respect

And that's just the start of my list.

In my opinion, you will never make a success of any business endeavour without possessing these values and characteristics.

And for me, it's morals over money every time. All the time.

That's how I win. That's how you win. That's how we all win.

So let me add one other thing that business is about: it's about doing the work.

When you come from nothing, growing up on a council estate, with no one owning their own home, no one earning much more than minimum wage, no one going to university and no one with any financial means to give you a leg-up . . .

You have to give yourself a leg-up.

You have to do the work. You can't just wake up and cruise through the day. You can't go to the gym at eleven o'clock, then scroll through Facebook pretending to do the work while actually doing very little.

You have to show up. For yourself. And for others.

WE ARE ALL MADE FOR MORE

No one becomes great on their own. No one.

As you go through life, you want to seek out people who believe in you. Who make you think. Who make you happy. Who challenge you to become the best version of yourself. The ones who show up when you're in need. The people who genuinely care.

> 'THE ONES WHO FAN YOUR FLAMES.'
>
> **- RUMI**

We are not supposed to take this journey of life alone; we are social creatures. We are best when we find our pack. We want to be surrounded by people who raise our standards and champion our dreams. Who believe in us even when we don't believe in ourselves. The ones who make walking the tightrope of life easier because, when we look down, we can see them. They are our safety net.

They listen to our crazy ideas and cheer us on. When things don't go right, they pick us up and dust us down. Then tell us to get back up and go again.

They won't always tell us what we want to hear, but they will tell us what we need to hear. They will go to war for us and with us. They will catch us when we fall.

These are the ones worth cherishing and holding tight.

I know that many people reading this might be thinking, *But where do I find these people?* The truth is, you start by being one. It's not the size of your pack that matters, it's the strength. Put yourself out for the people in your life. Go the extra mile . . . often. In an age when it's all too easy to try to maintain friendships over text messaging, be the one who picks up the phone, who jumps in the car and drives over. Show that you care.

To be happy and successful in life, you do not need to be surrounded by wealthy people; you need to be surrounded by people who are rich in their love for you.

If there is one piece of advice I could give over everything else, it is this. The quality of the people you allow in your life and who you allow to stay in your life will have a greater impact on you than anything else. If you want to fix your shit once and for all, take heed.

We are what we choose, the people who we let stay and the things that we keep.

ACKNOWLEDGEMENTS

Where do I start? There are so many people who have helped me fix my shit over the years that I could be here all day.

At the heart of everything I do is my son, Jett, without a doubt my greatest driving force. My North Star.

My wish is that he never has to fix any shit in his life, but, as that is a little unrealistic, I hope that I have helped equip him the best I can to handle it all. And, when in doubt, he knows Mum will always fight his corner. Come hell or high water. I'm so immensely proud of the young man he is becoming: smart, kind, brave, handsome and fiercely loyal. Just like his dad.

As for me, well I wouldn't be who I am without the two matri-archs in my life: my mum and my nan.

My nan, who just celebrated her ninety-fourth birthday as I write this, is my guiding light; simply the best human being I know. I have never known someone so universally loved by all who have crossed her path.

My mum taught me by example how to fix my shit, how to get back up and go again, no matter what life throws at you. As a nan, she knows no bounds; she has showered Jett with so much love, time, patience, adventures and beautiful childhood memories.

For all my friends, who provide me with the greatest gift any-one can give – a true support network. No matter how much shit I have going on in my life, I know for sure I never have to deal with it alone. I wish everyone could experience the surety this gives you.

For Joel, the ultimate publisher who believed in me from the jump and has continuously championed me at every turn. My agent, Scott Hoffman, who, although I am but a minnow in his pool, always make me feel like the killer whale! Having these two in my corner has given me the confidence to punch way above my weight.

For everyone in my team, who make taking the time out to write possible. Especially Matt Thomas, the best work husband I could wish for.

And yes, this is for you. The one I wrote it for. I hope it makes a difference. Once and for all.